I0417052

BUDGET
The United States
Department of the Interior

JUSTIFICATIONS

and Performance Information
Fiscal Year 2014

OFFICE OF THE
SPECIAL TRUSTEE FOR
AMERICAN INDIANS

NOTICE: These budget justifications are prepared for the Interior, Environment and Related Agencies Appropriations Subcommittees. Approval for release of the justifications prior to their printing in the public record of the Subcommittee hearings may be obtained through the Office of Budget of the Department of the Interior.

DEPARTMENT OF THE INTERIOR
OFFICE OF THE SPECIAL TRUSTEE
FOR AMERICAN INDIANS
BUDGET JUSTIFICATION
FOR FISCAL YEAR 2014

References to the *2013 Full Yr. CR* signify annualized amounts appropriated in P.L. 112-175, the Continuing Appropriations Act. These amounts are the 2012 enacted numbers annualized through the end of FY 2013 with a 0.612 percent across-the-board increase for discretionary programs. Exceptions to this include Wildland Fire Management, which received an anomaly in the 2013 CR to fund annual operations at $726.5 million. The *2013 Full Yr. CR* does not incorporate reductions associated with the Presidential sequestration order issued in accordance with section 251A of the Balanced Budget and Emergency Deficit Control Act, as amended (BBEDCA), 2 U.S.C. 109a. This column is provided for reference only.

DEPARTMENT OF THE INTERIOR
OFFICE OF THE SPECIAL TRUSTEE
FOR AMERICAN INDIANS
BUDGET JUSTIFICATION FOR FISCAL YEAR 2014

Table of Contents

Fiscal Year 2012 Annual Report to Congress

THIS PAGE INTENTIONALLY LEFT BLANK

Overview

Total 2014 Budget Request
(Dollars in Thousands)

Budget Authority	*2013 Full Yr. CR*	2012 Enacted	2014 Request
Current	*153,006*	152,075	139,677
Permanent	*413,163*	428,754	427,875
Total Current and Permanent	***566,169***	**580,829**	**567,552**
FTEs	*638*	*639*	*638*

Note: Current budget authority represents operating funds that are appropriated annually by Congress to the Office of the Special Trustee. Permanent budget authority represents certain funds held by DOI on behalf of Indian Tribes, some of which will be transferred to Tribes provided certain conditions are satisfied, and are considered U.S. Government funds.

Executive Summary

In FY 2014, the Department of the Interior will maintain its emphasis on providing services to the beneficiaries of the Indian trust. The Office of the Special Trustee for American Indians (OST) will continue its role in the oversight and operations of the fiduciary trust by monitoring trust reform in accordance with all applicable congressional actions and regulatory requirements. Proposed funding for OST supports the Department's Indian Fiduciary Trust Responsibilities.

The Congress has designated the Secretary of the Interior as the trustee delegate with responsibility for approximately 55 million surface acres of land, 57 million acres of subsurface mineral interests, and nearly $4.4 billion that is held in trust by the Federal Government on behalf of American Indians, Alaska Natives, and federally recognized Indian Tribes. OST's trust management of these assets includes conserving, maintaining, accounting, investing, disbursing, and reporting to individual Indians and federally recognized Tribes and tribal organizations on asset transactions generated from sales, leasing and other commercial activities on these lands.

Several significant events occurred in fiscal years 2012 and 2013 that impact OST and Indian Country both currently and in the foreseeable future. The Individual Indian Money Account Litigation Settlement (formerly referred to as the *Cobell v. Salazar* lawsuit), was authorized and confirmed by the Claims Resolution Act of 2010 and approved with finality on November 24, 2012. The settlement agreement included two classes: 1) the Historical Accounting class and, 2) the Trust Administration class. Payments to members of the Historical Accounting class are referred to as Stage I payments while payments to members of the Trust Administration class are referred to as Stage II payments; an individual may be a member of one or both classes. In December 2012, the Court appointed administrator began disbursing Stage I settlement payments, resulting in an exponential increase in inquiries to the Trust Beneficiary Call Center (TBCC) and requests for assistance from OST field office staff. The OST has a responsibility to locate Whereabouts Unknown (WAU) account holders as part of the settlement.

The Settlement also provides for a $1.9 billion Trust Land Consolidation Fund and charges the Department with the responsibility to use the Fund within a 10-year period to acquire, at fair market value, fractional interests in trust or restricted land from willing sellers individual Indian accountholders. Acquired interests will remain in trust or restricted status and be consolidated for beneficial use by tribal communities. The Secretary of the Interior established the Land Buy-Back Program for Tribal Nations to implement the land consolidation aspects of the Settlement. The OST will be responsible for completing all land appraisals required for the Buy-Back program. In addition, OST's TBCC has been designated the trust beneficiary point of contact for inquiries related to the hundreds of thousands of offers to purchase fractionated land across Indian Country.

In FY 2012, the Secretarial Commission on Indian Trust Administration and Reform established as the result of the Individual Indian Money Account Litigation Settlement, held three public meetings and has continued deliberations in FY 2013. The Commission's Charter expires in November of 2013, and requires submission of recommendations for potential improvements to the existing management and administration of the trust administration system. OST is working closely with the Commission and looks forward to receiving their recommendations in early FY 2014.

In FY 2012, OST received the results of the *Examination, Evaluation, and Recommendation Analysis of the Department of the Interior's Office of the Special Trustee for American Indians Study (Efficiency Study)* conducted by an independent third party and shared the report with the Congress, the Office of Management and Budget, the Secretary's management team, the Commission, and all OST employees. In 2012, OST submitted, and the Congress approved, a realignment of management responsibilities consistent with recommendations of the study. The Congress also approved funding reprogrammings in 2012. The 2014 budget is built on the 2012 enacted budget adjusted for approved reprogrammings. The Congress also approved a $946,000 transfer from Executive Directions to Program Operations and Support to take place in 2013. This is reported in the 2014 Internal Transfers column of the budget table. Implementation of "quick wins" identified in the study is in progress, with additional recommendations slated for implementation into FY 2014. OST anticipates that recommendations from the Commission and the *Efficiency Study* will both improve efficiencies in the delivery of fiduciary trust services to beneficiaries.

OST participates in the Tribal Interior Budget Council (TIBC), which provides a forum and a process for tribal representatives to advise OST on priority needs in Indian Country, thus facilitating tribal participation in OST budget formulation. TIBC meetings further provide an opportunity to inform Tribes on the status of Indian Country initiatives throughout the Federal Government.

Trust Management Reform

Milestones attained in trust management reform in recent years have allowed OST and the Bureau of Indian Affairs (BIA) to realize significant productivity efficiencies, and further improvements are in process. In FY 2012, OST launched an automated electronic notification to beneficiaries of funds deposited to their accounts. This notification provides beneficiaries a timely assurance that their funds are available to them. For the first time, the *Fiscal Year 2012 Annual Report to Congress* is included within the budget justification: please reference the last tab in this justification for additional details regarding OST's accomplishments and successes relative to trust reform.

Historical Trust Accounting

In 1994, Congress passed *The American Indian Trust Fund Management Reform Act of 1994* (P. L. 103-412; 108 Stat. 4239; U.S.C. 4001 et seq.) (the "1994 Act") and established the Office of the Special Trustee for American Indians. The 1994 Act requires, in part, the Secretary of the Interior to "account for the daily and annual balance of all funds held in trust by the United States for the benefit of an Indian Tribe or an individual Indian which are deposited or invested pursuant to the Act of June 24, 1938 (25 U.S.C. 162a)." In July 2001, the Office of Historical Trust Accounting (OHTA) was created by Secretarial Order to plan, organize, direct, and execute the historical accounting of Individual Indian Money (IIM) accounts OHTA's responsibilities were later expanded in 2002 to include the provision of historical accountings for tribal accounts.

OHTA's management model is based on a small staff of federal employees directing the efforts of a number of contractors. Contractors have provided critical technical expertise in areas such as accounting services, historical research, information resources, data security, statistical analysis, document search, collection, and reproduction. OHTA currently supports resolution of lawsuits filed by or on behalf of 66 Tribes as of March 1, 2013. These cases are in various Federal District Courts and/or the Court of Federal Claims.

Organizational Chart

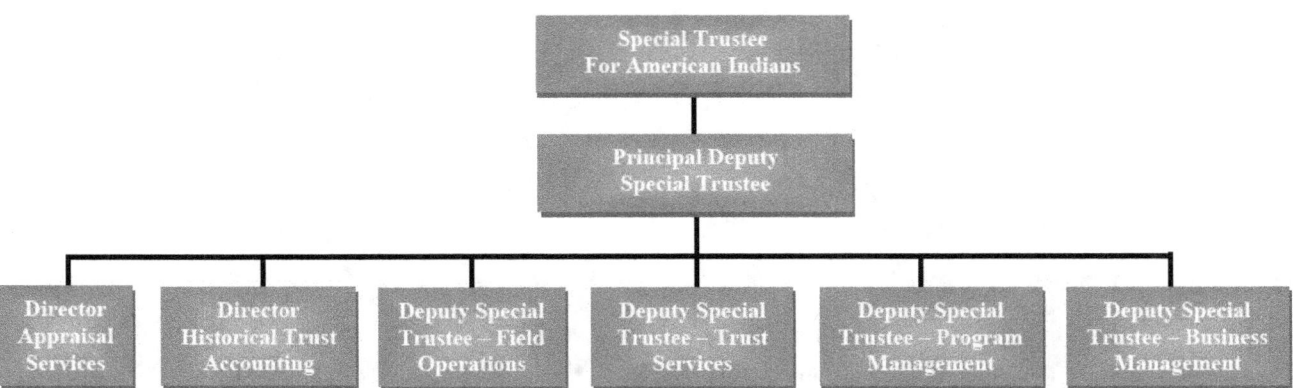

Analysis of Budgetary Changes
Office of the Special Trustee
For American Indians

FY 2012 to FY 2014 Changes	2014	
	$000	FTE
Office of the Special Trustee 2012 Enacted	152,075	639
Programmatic Changes	**-11,005**	**-1**
Executive Direction	**-1,865**	**-27**
Program reduction and eliminations	*-1,865*	*-27*
Program Operations and Support	***-9,140***	***+26***
Program Operations	-10,893	+7
Field Operations	+143	+11
Program Enhancement	*+143*	
Appraisal Services	-11	+3
Savings due to efficiencies	*-11*	
Trust Services	-207	+5
Elimination of Internship Program	*-207*	*+*
Historical Trust Accounting	-6,986	+1
Reduction in Contracts	*-6,986*	
Trust Accountability	-3,832	-13
Program Completion	*-3,832*	
Program Support	**+1,753**	**+19**
Business Management	+197	+16
Expanded Operational Workload	*+353*	
IT Transformation	*+190*	
Elimination of Inter-Tribal Monitoring Association Grant	*-346*	
Program Management	+1,556	+3
Program Reduction-Trust Records	*-246*	
Program Enhancement-Trust Review and Audit	*+1,802*	
Fixed Cost Changes	**-1,393**	**0**
TOTAL, Federal Trust Programs 2014	**139,677**	**638**

FY 2014 Budget Request

The mission of OST is to fulfill its fiduciary trust responsibilities to American Indian Tribes, individual Indians and Alaska natives by incorporating a beneficiary focus and beneficiary participation while providing effective, competent stewardship and management of trust assets. In 2014 OST will continue to its efforts to improve the delivery of services to Indian beneficiaries with increased efficiency and transparency.

Key 2014 priorities are summarized below:

- Manage $3.7 billion in Tribal funds and $728 million in Individual Indian Money (IIM) funds (including receipting, investing, disbursing, accounting, and reporting).
- Continue to reduce the number of Whereabouts Unknown (WAU) account holders.
- Support and fund self-determination and self-governance contracts/compacts, e.g., appraisals and beneficiary processes programs.
- Provide historical analysis, research, and support for tribal trust litigation and settlement efforts.
- Perform appraisals for Indian land.
- Support the Secretarial Commission on Indian Trust Administration and Reform established by Secretarial Order 3292, including working with the Commission's management consultant to complete its Department-wide assessment of the Trust Administration System.
- Support implementation of the Individual Indian Money Account Litigation Settlement payout process by:
  - Completing all of the appraisals of land for offers made in FY 2014
  - Locating WAU account holders
  - Addressing beneficiary concerns and updating account information via the TBCC
  - Conducting outreach
  - Handling telephone inquiries through the TBCC and in-person inquiries in the field
  - Printing and mailing of offers to purchase fractionated land

Please reference individual program budget justifications for OST's complete program of work for 2014.

OST's FY 2014 discretionary budget request is $139.7 million, a decrease of $12.4 million from the 2012 enacted budget level. The requested funding level reflects the following savings and changes:
1. Executive Direction - program reduction of -$1.9 million which includes:
   - $727,000 reduction for the National Indian Program Training Center contract
   - $907,000 million reduction for Trust Regulations, Policies, and Procedures
   - $231,000 for the elimination of the Product Development Initiative

2. $3.8 million reduction through the elimination of the Trust Accountability division. As certain trust reform projects were completed, on-going functions and personnel resources were realigned into other OST offices. Trust training ($1.8M), and product development ($1M) were eliminated. As a result of the consolidation of probate offices, and savings from the digitization of its probate records, funding for the Office of Hearings and Appeals was reduced by $1.0 million.

3. $7.0 million reduction in the Office of Historical Accounting (OHTA) that includes contract reductions for litigation support due to recent tribal settlements.

4. $197,000 increase for Business Management for cost increases in services for Human Resources, Acquisitions, Financial Accounting, and OST wide-training through a partnership with DOI University.

5. $246,000 savings in the Office of Trust Records as a result of increased efficiencies and savings in overhead.

6. $207,000 savings in Trust Services from the elimination of the Internship program and from improved efficiencies through the development of an application program that reduces manual entry requirements.

7. $1.6 million net increase to Program Management composed of an increase of $1.8 million for Trust Review and Audit to conduct additional examinations, which is partially off-set by a reduction of $246,000 in the Office of Trust Records.

8. $1.4 million reduction in fixed costs, primarily through the consolidation and elimination of office space in FY2013, and additional planned reductions in FY2014.

Base Budget Analysis

OST's FY 2014 base budget was developed using analysis of historical execution, determination of changing requirements, projection of operating costs, emphasis on current initiatives and priorities, and the anticipated completion of certain trust reform efforts.

As part of this analysis, OST utilizes Activity-Based Cost Management (ABC/M) data to make organizational assessments and align work efforts with Government Performance and Results Act of 1993 (GPRA) goals. ABC/M is being used to assist managers in cost estimating, cost forecasting and improving programs by identifying future cost avoidance and efficiency savings.

Data Verification and Validation

The OST Risk Management program utilizes a three pronged approach to ensure that data and reports produced from OST programs are accurate, efficient, and timely. The approach includes: 1) program managers' annual self-assessments and OMB Circular A-123, Appendix A transaction testing, 2) Office of Trust Review and Audit - Risk Management internal reviews (internal performance audits), and may include 3) annual independent Office of Inspector General audits (performed by KPMG currently) in accordance with the Reform Act and U.S. Government Accountability Office reviews and audits.

OST has implemented data procedures compliant with the "Data Verification and Validation (V&V) Assessment Matrix" guidance issued by the Assistant Secretary for Policy Management and Budget on January 16, 2003, for performance data that is collected and submitted. Primary responsibility for data quality resides with the designated senior manager for the performance measure. The responsible manager has designated a program official as the data point of contact. The data point of contact is responsible for the collection of data, reporting of data, and conducting an annual assessment based upon the Department's Data V&V assessment guidance.

Secretarial Initiatives

The FY 2014 President's Budget Request includes $68,000 for OST's participation in the Department's IT Transformation efforts through the Department's Working Capital Fund. These funds will support IT Transformation project-level planning and coordination and the implementation of enterprise IT.

Administration's Management Agenda

Enterprise Reforms

The Department of the Interior supports the President's Management Agenda to cut waste and implement a government that is more responsive and open. The OST budget supports the Department's plan to build upon the Accountable Government Initiative through a set of integrated enterprise reforms designed to support collaborative, evidence-based resource management decisions; efficient Information Technology (IT) Transformation; optimized programs, business processes, and facilities; and a network of innovative cost controlling measures that leverage strategic workforce alignment to realize an effective 21st Century Interior organization.

Campaign to Cut Waste

Over the last three years, the Administration has implemented a series of management reforms to curb uncontrolled growth in contract spending, terminate poorly performing information technology projects, deploy state of the art fraud detection tools, focus agency leaders on achieving ambitious improvements in high-priority areas, and open government up to the public to increase accountability and accelerate innovation.

In November 2011, President Obama issued an Executive Order reinforcing these performance and management reforms and the achievement of efficiencies and cost-cutting across the government. This Executive Order identifies specific savings as part of the Administration's Campaign to Cut Waste to achieve a 20 percent reduction in administrative spending from 2010 to 2013 and sustain these savings in 2014. Each agency is directed to establish a plan to reduce the combined costs associated with travel, employee information technology devices, printing, executive fleet services, and extraneous promotional items and other areas.

The Department of the Interior is on target to reduce administrative spending by $217 million from 2010 levels by the end of 2013, and to sustain these savings in 2014. To meet this goal, the Department is leading efforts to reduce waste and create efficiencies by reviewing projected and actual administrative spending to allocate efficiency targets for Bureaus and Departmental Offices to achieve the 20 percent target. Additional details on the Campaign to Cut Waste can be found at http://www.whitehouse.gov/the-press-office/2011/11/09/executive-order-promoting-efficient-spending.

Real Property

In support of the Administration's real property cost savings efforts, the Department issued a policy restricting the maximum amount of Bureau/Office-leased and GSA-provided space to FY 2010 levels and reducing the target utilization rate (sq. ft. per person) for office space by 10 percent. Through actions such as consolidations, collocations, and disposals, OST plans to achieve a utilization rate of 180 usable sq. ft. per person by the end of FY 2014.

Data Center Consolidation

As part of the Administration's Management Priorities, the Department has initiated a plan for Information Technology (IT) Transformation designed to reduce spending by the consolidation of IT infrastructure and services under a single Chief Information Officer (CIO). The new IT shared services organization will transform the way that IT is delivered to over 70,000 DOI employees, using advances in technology to provide better services for less. OST supports the Department's initiative to reduce 95 data centers by FY 2015 without disruption to mission.

2014 Strategic Objective Performance Summary

In FY 2010, the Department updated the Strategic Plan in light of the Administration's priorities, goals, and objectives; recent innovations and efficiencies in delivering mission objectives; and the goal to provide a more integrated and focused approach to track performance across a wide range of DOI programs. Although many of the outcome goals and performance measures remain consistent from the previous Strategic Plan, the organizing principles for those goals and measures reflect the new approach to meeting the Department's mission responsibilities. Budget and program plans for FY 2014 are fully consistent with the goals, outcomes, and measures described in the FY 2011 – 2016 version of the DOI Strategic Plan. OST's Strategic Plan measures are discussed below and presented in the following table.

OST's three Strategic Plan performance measures are key components of the Department's strategy for achieving the goal of Meeting Trust, Treaty, and Other Responsibilities to American Indians and Alaska Natives by fulfilling DOI's fiduciary trust. Considerable efforts and dollars are devoted to managing Indian fiduciary assets, reforming processes, and improving performance. The Department works to ensure that technical and economic assistance is provided to the Tribes, and that organizational and process changes are introduced to address longstanding issues. OST contributes significantly to the Department's achievements through continual improvements in processes that improve efficiency and by achieving or surpassing performance goals. The three OST Strategic Plan measures are:

- *Percent timeliness of financial account information provided to trust beneficiaries.*
  The percent of timeliness numerator is based on the number of printed and mailed trust beneficiaries account statements divided by the denominator, which is the total number of statements to be mailed. The unit cost of providing timely financial account information to trust beneficiaries is derived by dividing the cost of printing and mailing the account statements by the number of statements mailed per year. OST has demonstrated sustained performance of 100 percent for the last five years for this measure.

- *Percent of financial information initially processed accurately in Trust beneficiaries' accounts.* This measure is also identified as OST's Key Performance Indicator (KPI). The unit cost of a transaction is derived by dividing the total cost of processing transactions by the number of transactions for the year (denominator). Increases in the total number of transactions per year (denominator) are estimated based on historical trends from previous years.

  To achieve the Secretary's Indian Fiduciary Trust Responsibilities, OST ensures that financial information initially is processed accurately in trust beneficiaries' accounts at least 99 percent of the time, and has demonstrated sustained performance of 100 percent for the last three years for this measure. OST has established a system of internal controls to ensure that posted transactions are complete and accurate. Additionally, OST monitors processing times to provide assurance that transactions are posted within the targeted timeframes and continually evaluates and refines the system of internal controls. Approximately 816,000 statements are expected to be printed and mailed during FY 2014.

- ***Percent of oil and gas revenue transmitted by ONRR recorded in the Trust Funds Accounting System (TFAS) within 24 hours of receipt.***
  The unit cost for recording revenue in TFAS consists of the portion of the employee's time devoted to this duty divided by the number of business days (usually around 250) on which this function is performed. OST has demonstrated sustained performance of 100 percent for the last three years for this measure.

KEY TO CODES:

Target Codes: SP = Strategic Plan measures
APG = Agency Priority Goal
BUR = Bureau specific measure

Type Codes: C = Cumulative Measure

UNK = Prior year data unavailable
n/a = information is unknown or cannot be determined at this time

A = Annual Measure

Mission Area 3: Advance Government-to-Government Relationships with Indian Nations and Alaska Natives and Honor Commitments to Insular Areas

Goal #1: Meet Our Trust, Treaty, and Other Responsibilities to American Indians and Alaska Natives

Supporting Performance Measures	TYPE	PY-3 Actual	PY-2 Actual	PY-1 Actual	PY Plan	PY Actual	CY Plan	BY Budget Request	Long-Term Target 2016
Strategy #2: Fulfill Fiduciary Trust									
Percent of financial information initially processed accurately in trust beneficiaries' accounts. (SP)	A	99.9%	100.0%	100.0%	99.0%	99.99%	99.0%	99.0%	99.0%
		8,262,510	8,485,028	8,342,464	8,415,000	8,803,464	8,464,500	8,514,000	8,514,000
Contributing Programs: Trust Services		8,267,407	8,487,311	8,344,261	8,500,000	8,804,688	8,550,000	8,600,000	8,600,000
Percent timeliness of financial account information provided to trust beneficiaries. (SP)	A	100.0%	100.0%	100.0%	99.5%	100.0%	100.0%	100.0%	100.0%
		770,198	787,340	764,553	796,000	786,838	800,000	816,000	816,000
Contributing Programs: Trust Services		770,198	787,340	764,553	800,000	786,838	800,000	816,000	816,000
Timeliness of Mineral Revenue Payments to American Indians: Percent of oil and gas revenue transmitted by ONRR recorded in the Trust Funds Accounting System within 24 hours of receipt. (SP)	A	99.9%	100.0%	100.0%	99.1%	100.0%	99.1%	99.0%	99.0%
		102,505,538	154,282,290	280,287,244	153,650,000	372,372,320	153,650,000	277,200,000	277,200,000
Contributing Programs: Budget, Finance & Administration and Information Resource									
Contributing Programs: Trust Services		102,618,230	154,282,290	280,287,244	155,000,000	372,372,320	155,000,000	280,000,000	280,000,000

TAB INSERT

Bureau Level Tables

Office of the Special Trustee for American Indians
Federal Trust Programs
FY 2014 President's Budget
($000)

Activities	FTEs	2013 Operating Plan	2012 Enacted	Approved Reprogramming 1/	Adjusted 2012 Enacted	FY 2014 Fixed Costs	FY 2014 Internal Transfers 2/	FY 2014 Program changes	FY 2014 President's Budget
EXECUTIVE DIRECTION	6	3,315	2,212	2,834	5,046	5	-1,160	-1,865	2,026
PROGRAM OPERATIONS AND SUPPORT	632	149,691	149,863	-2,834	147,029	-1,398	1,160	-9,140	137,651
PROGRAM OPERATIONS	440	96,844	110,492	-3,021	107,471	392	-9,488	-10,893	87,482
Field Operations	225	26,278	23,433		23,433	198	973	143	24,747
Appraisal Services	71	10,755	10,691		10,691	64	0	-11	10,744
Trust Services	124	28,690	27,661	-946	26,715	112	2,326	-207	28,946
Historical Trust Accounting	20	31,121	31,121		31,121	18	-1,108	-6,986	23,045
Trust Accountability	0		17,586	-2,075	15,511	0	-11,679	-3,832	0
PROGRAM SUPPORT	192	52,847	39,371	187	39,558	-1,790	10,648	1,753	50,169
Business Management	87	39,990	21,752	187	21,939	-1,884	14,454	197	34,706
Program Management	105	12,857	17,619		17,619	94	-3,806	1,556	15,463
FEDERAL TRUST PROGRAMS TOTAL	638	153,006	152,075	0	152,075	-1,393	0	-11,005	139,677

1/ Congress approved reprogramming proposed in August 14, 2012 letter.

2/ Congress approved a $946,000 internal transfer from Executive Direction to Program Operations proposed in August 14, 2012 letter.

Budget at a Glance
Federal Trust Programs
(Dollars in thousands)

	2013 Full Year CR	2012 Enacted	Fixed Costs	Internal Transfers	Program Changes	2014 Request
EXECUTIVE DIRECTION	3,315	5,046	+5	-1,160	-1,865	2,026
Program reduction and eliminations		N/A			[-1,865]	
PROGRAM OPERATIONS AND SUPPORT						
PROGRAM OPERATIONS						
Field Operations	26,278	23,433	+198	+973	+143	24,747
Program Enhancement		N/A			[+143]	
Appraisal Services	10,755	10,691	+64	+0	-11	10,744
Savings due to efficiencies		N/A			[-11]	
Trust Services	28,690	26,715	+112	+2,326	-207	28,946
Elimination of Internship Program.		N/A			[-207]	
Historical Trust Accounting	31,121	31,121	+18	-1,108	-6,986	23,045
Reduction in contracts		N/A			[-6,986]	
Trust Accountability	0	15,511	+0	-11,679	-3,832	0
Program Completion		N/A			[-3,832]	
Activity Total, Program Operations	96,844	107,471	392	-9,488	-10,893	87,482
PROGRAM SUPPORT						
Business Management	39,990	21,939	-1,884	+14,454	+197	34,706
Expanded Operational Workload		N/A			[+353]	
IT Transformation		N/A			[+190]	
Elimination of Inter-Tribal Monitoring		N/A			[-346]	
Program Management	12,857	17,619	+94	-3,806	+1,556	15,463
Program Reduction-Trust Records		N/A			[-246]	
Program Enhancement-Trust Review and Audit		N/A			[+1,802]	
Activity Total, Program Support	52,847	39,558	-1,790	+10,648	+1,753	50,169
TOTAL, Federal Trust Programs	153,006	152,075	-1,393	+0	-11,005	139,677

Summary of Requirements
(Dollars in Thousands)

Federal Trust Programs

	2013 Full Year CR	2012 Enacted		Fixed Costs & Related	Internal Transfers 2/	Program Changes (+/-)		2014 Request		Change from PY	
	Amount	Total FTE 1/	Amount			FTE	Amount	FTE	Amount	FTE	Amount
EXECUTIVE DIRECTION	3,315	33	5,046	+5	-1,160	-27	-1,865	6	2,026	-27	-3,020
PROGRAM OPERATIONS AND SUPPORT											
PROGRAM OPERATIONS											
Field Operations	26,278	206	23,433	+198	+973	+11	+143	217	24,747	+11	+1,314
Appraisal Services	10,755	68	10,691	+64	+0	+3	-11	71	10,744	+3	+53
Trust Services	28,690	119	26,715	+112	+2,326	+5	-207	124	28,946	+5	+2,231
Historical Trust Accounting	31,121	19	31,121	+18	-1,108	+1	-6,986	20	23,045	+1	-8,076
Trust Accountability	0	13	15,511	+0	-11,679	-13	-3,832	0	0	-13	-15,511
Total, Program Operations	**96,844**	**426**	**107,471**	**392**	**-9,488**	**6**	**-10,893**	**432**	**87,482**	**6**	**-19,989**
PROGRAM SUPPORT											
Business Management	39,990	72	21,939	-1,884	+14,454	+16	+197	88	34,706	+16	+12,767
Program Management	12,857	109	17,619	+94	-3,806	+3	+1,556	112	15,463	+3	-2,156
Total, Program Support	**52,847**	**181**	**39,558**	**-1,790**	**+10,648**	**+19**	**+1,753**	**200**	**50,169**	**+19**	**+10,611**
TOTAL, Federal Trust Programs	**153,006**	**639**	**152,075**	**-1,393**	**+0**	**-1**	**-11,005**	**638**	**139,677**	**-1**	**-12,398**

1/ 2012 FTE amounts reflect actual usage, not 2012 enacted formulation estimates.

2/ Congress approved a $946,000 internal transfer from Executive Direction to Program Operations proposed in August 14, 2012 letter.

Office of the Special Trustee for American Indians
Justification of Fixed Costs and Internal Realignments
(Dollars in Thousands)

Other Fixed Cost Changes and Projections	2012 Total	2012 Enacted to 2014 Request Change
Change in Number of Paid Days	+0	+260
The combined fixed cost estimate includes an adjustment for one additional paid day between FY2012 and FY 2013. The number of paid days does not change between FY2013 and FY2014.		
Pay Raise	+0	+670
The PY column reflects the total pay raise changes as reflected in the PY President's Budget. The BY Change column reflects the total pay raise changes between FY2012-FY2014.		
Employer Share of Federal Health Benefit Plans	+0	+308
The change reflects expected increases in employer's share of Federal Health Benefit Plans.		
Departmental Working Capital Fund	+15	-72
The change reflects expected changes in the charges for centrally billed Department services and other services through the Working Capital Fund. These charges are displayed in the Budget Justification for Department Management.		
Worker's Compensation Payments	+60	-64
The adjustment is for changes in the costs of compensating injured employees and dependents of employees who suffer accidental deaths while on duty. Costs for the BY will reimburse the Department of Labor, Federal Employees Compensation Fund, pursuant to 5 U.S.C. 8147(b) as amended by Public Law 94-273.		
Unemployment Compensation Payments	+0	+0
The adjustment is for projected changes in the costs of unemployment compensation claims to be paid to the Department of Labor, Federal Employees Compensation Account, in the Unemployment Trust Fund, pursuant to Public Law 96-499.		
GSA Rental Payments	+602	-2,495
The adjustment is for changes in the costs payable to General Services Administration (GSA) and others resulting from changes in rates for office and non-office space as estimated by GSA, as well as the rental costs of other currently occupied space. These costs include building security; in the case of GSA space, these are paid to Department of Homeland Security (DHS). Costs of mandatory office relocations, i.e. relocations in cases where due to external events there is no alternative but to vacate the currently occupied space, are also included.		

Internal Realignments and Non-Policy/Program Changes (Net-Zero)	2014 Request (+/-)	
Internal transfer from Executive Direction to External Affairs	+/-	187
Internal transfer from Executive Direction to Field Operations	+/-	973
Internal transfer from Trust Records to Budget, Finance and Administration.	+/-	3,986
Internal transfer from Trust Review & Audit to Business Management	+/-	1,565
Internal transfer from Trust Accountability to Budget, Finance and Administration.	+/-	8,716
Internal transfer from Trust Accountability to Trust Review and Audit.	+/-	637
Internal transfer from Trust Accountability to Trust Services.	+/-	2,326
Internal transfer from Budget, Finance and Administration to External Affairs.	+/-	350
Internal transfer from Historical Accounting to Trust Records.	+/-	1,108

MAX Tables/Budget Schedules

(Dollars in Thousands)

	Treasury Account ID: 14 – 0120 – 0	FY 2012 Actual	FY 2013 Estimate	FY 2014 Estimate
	Obligations by program activity:			
0001	Program operations, support, and improvements	145	151	138
0002	Executive direction	4	2	2
0900	Total new obligations	149	153	140
	Budgetary Resources:			
	Unobligated balance:			
1000	Unobligated balance brought forward, Oct 1	5	12	15
1021	Recoveries of prior year unpaid obligations	4	2	2
1050	Unobligated balance (total)	9	14	17
	Budget authority:			
	Appropriations, discretionary:			
1100	Appropriation	152	153	140
1160	Appropriation, discretionary (total)	152	153	140
	Spending authority from offsetting collections, discretionary:			
1701	Change in uncollected payments, Federal Sources	0	1	1
1750	Spending authority from offsetting collections, disc (total)	0	1	1
1900	Budget authority (total)	152	154	141
1930	Total budgetary resources available	161	168	158
	Memorandum (non-add) entries:			
1941	Unexpired unobligated balance, end of year	12	15	18
	Change in obligated balance:			
	Unpaid Obligations:			
3000	Unpaid obligations, brought forward, Oct 1	37	43	34
3010	Obligations incurred, unexpired accounts	149	153	140
3020	Outlays (gross)	-139	-160	-144
3040	Recoveries of prior year unpaid obligations, unexpired	-4	-2	-2
3050	Unpaid obligations, end of year	43	34	28
	Uncollected payments:			
3060	Uncollected paymts, Fed Sources, brought forward, Oct 1	-1	0	0
3070	Change in uncollected pymts, Fed Sources, unexpired	0	-1	-1
3071	Change in uncollected pymts, Fed sources, expired	1	1	1
3090	Uncollected pymts, Fed Sources, end of year	0	0	0
	Memorandum (non-add) entries:			
3100	Obligated balance, start of year	36	43	34
3200	Obligated balance, end of year	43	34	28
	Budget authority and outlays, net:			
	Discretionary:			
4000	Budget authority, gross	152	154	141
	Outlays, gross:			
4010	Outlays from new discretionary authority	104	123	113
4011	Outlays from discretionary balances	35	37	31
4020	Outlays, gross (total)	139	160	144
	Offsets against gross budget authority and outlays:			
	Offsetting collections (collected) from:			
4030	Federal sources	-2	-1	-1
	Additional offsets against gross budget authority only:			
4050	Change in uncollected pymts, Fed sources, unexpired	0	-1	-1
4052	Offsetting collections credited to expired accounts	2	1	1
4060	Additional offsets against budget authority only (total):	2	0	0
4070	Budget authority, net (discretionary)	152	153	140
4080	Outlays, net (discretionary)	137	159	143
4180	Budget authority, net (total)	152	153	140
4190	Outlays, net (total)	137	159	143

Note: Table may not add due to rounding.

Object Classification

(Dollars in millions)

	Treasury Account ID: 14 – 0120 – 0	FY 2012 Actual	FY 2013 Estimate	FY 2014 Estimate
	Object Classification			
	Direct obligations			
	Personnel compensation			
1111	Full time permanent	45	47	47
1113	Other than full-time permanent	1	1	1
1115	Other personnel compensation	1	2	2
1119	Total personnel compensation	47	50	50
1121	Civilian personnel benefits	14	13	13
1210	Travel and transportation of persons	2	3	3
1231	Rental Payments to GSA	1	3	3
1232	Rental Payments to others	3	6	6
1233	Communications, utilities, and miscellaneous charges	1	2	2
1251	Advisory and assistance services	4	17	14
1252	Other services from non-federal sources	45	27	18
1253	Other goods and services from federal sources	13	13	12
1260	Supplies and Materials	1	1	1
1310	Equipment	2	2	2
1990	Subtotal, obligations, Direct obligations	133	137	124
	Reimbursable obligations			
2252	Reimbursable obligations: Other Services from non-Federal sources	3	3	3
	Allocation Account - direct:			
	Personnel compensation:			
3111	Full-time permanent	6	6	6
3113	Other than full-time permanent	2	2	2
3119	Total personnel compensation	8	8	8
3121	Civilian personnel benefits	2	2	2
3231	Rental payments to GSA	1	1	1
3252	Other services from non-federal sources	2	2	2
3990	Subtotal, obligations, Allocation Account - direct	13	13	13
9999	Total new obligations	149	153	140

Note: Table may not add due to rounding.

(Dollars in millions)

	Treasury Account ID: 14 – 5265 – 0	FY 2012 Actual	FY 2013 Estimate	FY 2014 Estimate
	Obligations by program activity			
0001	Direct program activity	361	363	340
0900	Total new obligations (object class 41.0)	361	363	340
	Budgetary Resources:			
	Unobligated balance:			
1000	Unobligated balance brought forward, Oct 1	116	66	16
	Budget authority:			
	Appropriations, mandatory:			
1201	Appropriations [-5265]	311	313	324
1260	Appropriations, mandatory (total)	311	313	324
1930	Total budgetary resources available	427	379	340
	Memorandum (non-add) entries:			
1941	Unexpired unobligated balance, end of year	66	16	0
	Change in obligated balance:			
	Unpaid obligations:			
3000	Unpaid obligations, brought forward, Oct 1	0	0	50
3010	Obligations incurred, unexpired accounts	361	363	340
3020	Outlays (gross)	-361	-313	-324
3050	Unpaid Obligations, end of year	0	50	66
	Memorandum (non-add) entries:			
3100	Obligated balance, start of year	0	0	50
3200	Obligated balance, end of year	0	50	66
	Budget authority and outlays, net:			
	Mandatory:			
4090	Budget authority, gross	311	313	324
	Outlays, gross:			
4100	Outlays from new mandatory authority	0	300	311
4101	Outlays from mandatory balances	361	13	13
4110	Outlays, gross (total)	361	313	324
4160	Budget authority, net (mandatory)	311	313	324
4170	Outlays, net (mandatory)	361	313	324
4180	Budget authority, net (total)	311	313	324
4190	Outlays, net (total)	361	313	324
	Memorandum (non-add) entries:			
5000	Total investments, SOY: Federal securities: Par value	116	66	125
5001	Total investments, EOY: Federal securities: Par value	66	125	128
5010	Total investments, SOY: non-Fed securities: Market value	412	464	472
5011	Total investments, EOY: non-Fed securities: Market value	464	472	483

Note: Table may not add due to rounding.

(Dollars in millions)

	Treasury Account ID: 14 – 8030 – 0	FY 2012 Actual	FY 2013 Estimate	FY 2014 Estimate
	Obligations by program activity			
0001	Direct program activity	118	121	123
0900	Total new obligations	118	121	123
	Budgetary Resources:			
	Unobligated balance:			
1000	Unobligated balance brought forward, Oct 1	58	40	19
	Budget authority:			
	Appropriations, mandatory:			
1201	Appropriations, mandatory: [-8030]	100	100	104
1260	Appropriations, mandatory (total)	100	100	104
1930	Total budgetary resources available	158	140	123
	Memorandum (non-add) entries:			
1941	Unexpired unobligated balance, end of year	40	19	0
	Change in obligated balance:			
	Unpaid Obligations			
3000	Unpaid obligations, brought forward, Oct 1	0	0	21
3010	Obligations incurred, unexpired accounts	118	121	123
3020	Outlays (gross)	-118	-100	-104
3050	Unpaid obligations, end of year	0	21	40
	Memorandum (non-add) entries:			
3100	Obligated balance, start of year	0	0	21
3200	Obligated balance, end of year	0	21	40
	Budget authority and outlays, net:			
	Mandatory:			
4090	Budget authority, gross	100	100	104
	Outlays, gross:			
4100	Outlays from new mandatory authority	0	94	98
4101	Outlays from mandatory balances	118	6	6
4110	Outlays, gross (total)	118	100	104
4160	Budget authority, net (mandatory)	100	100	104
4170	Outlays, net (mandatory)	118	100	104
4180	Budget authority, net (total)	100	100	104
4190	Outlays, net (total)	118	100	104
	Memorandum (non-add) entries:			
5000	Total investments, SOY: Federal securities: Par value	58	40	61
5001	Total investments, EOY: Federal securities: Par value	40	61	63
5010	Total investments, SOY: non-Fed securities: Market value	108	125	127
5011	Total investments, EOY: non-Fed securities: Market value	125	127	130

Note: Table may not add due to rounding.

Office of the Special Trustee for American Indians
Employee Count by Grade

(Total Employment)

		FY 2012 Actuals	FY 2013 Estimate	FY 2014 Estimate
Executive Level II		0	0	1
SES		11	10	10
	Subtotal	11	10	11
SL - 00		0	0	0
ST - 00		0	0	0
	Subtotal	0	0	0
GS/GM -15		37	37	35
GS/GM -14		108	104	104
GS/GM -13		94	90	91
GS -12		50	50	50
GS -11		27	27	27
GS -10		0	0	0
GS - 9		30	30	30
GS - 8		22	23	23
GS -7		164	164	164
GS - 6		36	41	41
GS - 5		52	58	58
GS - 4		39	35	35
GS - 3		0	0	0
GS - 2		0	0	0
GS -1		0	0	0
	Subtotal	659	659	658
Other Pay Schedule Systems		1	1	1
Total employment (actuals & estimates)		**671**	**670**	**670**

Section 405 Compliance

OST adheres to the requirements of Section 405 contained in the Department of the Interior, Environment and Related Agencies Appropriations Act, 2010, requiring agencies to present in their annual budget justification, any external and internal administrative costs, overhead charges, deductions, reserves, or holdbacks from programs, projects, and activities to support government-wide, Departmental, and OST administrative functions or headquarters, regional, or central office operations.

OST generally budgets for these support costs in the Budget, Finance, and Administration (BF&A) line item within the Business Management division in the Program Support subactivity. The largest of these centralized costs includes funding for Human Resources, space, and working capital fund activities. OST plans to charge the Federal Trust Programs' budgets for costs associated with centralized service contracts for security, Human Resources, Acquisitions, and Accounting support. These charges are allocated based on either the number of people in each program, funds obligated, or the program's percentage of transactions. Space costs at the Department's Main Interior Building (MIB) will be charged based on square feet utilized by those programs located at the MIB.

	2014 Estimate
Working Capital Fund Administrative Costs	
WCF Centralized Billings	$1,578,300
WCF Direct Billings	$3,561,500
Total WCF Costs	**$5,139,800**

Of the WCF Direct Billings, those charges related to Information Resources are charged directly to that program; all others are paid by BF&A.

External Administrative Costs	FY 2014
Human Resources Support	$1,248,000
Acquisition Support (included in WCF Centralized billing)	$1,763,500
Accounting Support (included in WCF Centralized billing)	$538,300
Security	$349,000
Space Rental	$1,580,630
Chargeback Estimate	**$5,479,430**

TAB INSERT

Language Citations

Appropriation Language

Federal Funds

Federal Trust Programs

(Including Transfer of Funds)

For the operation of trust programs for Indians by direct expenditure, contracts, cooperative agreements, compacts, and grants, $139,677,000, to remain available until expended, of which not to exceed $23,045,000, from this or any other Act, shall be available for historical accounting: Provided, That funds for trust management improvements and litigation support may, as needed, be transferred to or merged with the Bureau of Indian Affairs, "Operation of Indian Programs" account; the Office of the Solicitor, "Salaries and Expenses" account; and the Office of the Secretary, "Salaries and Expenses" account: Provided further, That funds made available through contracts or grants obligated during fiscal year 2014, as authorized by the Indian Self-Determination Act of 1975 (25 U.S.C. 450 et seq.), shall remain available until expended by the contractor or grantee: Provided further, That, notwithstanding any other provision of law, the statute of limitations shall not commence to run on any claim, including any claim in litigation pending on the date of the enactment of this Act, concerning losses to or mismanagement of trust funds, until the affected tribe or individual Indian has been furnished with an accounting of such funds from which the beneficiary can determine whether there has been a loss: Provided further, That, notwithstanding any other provision of law, the Secretary shall not be required to provide a quarterly statement of performance for any Indian trust account that has not had activity for at least 18 months and has a balance of $15.00 or less: Provided further, That the Secretary shall issue an annual account statement and maintain a record of any such accounts and shall permit the balance in each such account to be withdrawn upon the express written request of the account holder: Provided further, That not to exceed $50,000 is available for the Secretary to make payments to correct administrative errors of either disbursements from or deposits to Individual Indian Money or Tribal accounts after September 30, 2002: Provided further, That erroneous payments that are recovered shall be credited to and remain available in this account for this purpose.

Note: A full year 2013 appropriation for this account was not enacted at the time the budget was prepared; therefore, the budget assumes this account is operating under the Continuing Appropriations Resolution, 2013 (P.L. 112-175). The amounts included for 2013 reflect the annualized level provided by the continuing resolution.

Justification of Proposed Language Changes

None

Appropriation Language and Citations

1. For operation of trust programs for Indians by direct expenditure, contracts, cooperative agreements, compacts, and grants,

    - **25 U.S.C. 450(f)(a) and 450h(a)** directs the Secretary, upon the request of any Indian tribe, to enter into a contract or contracts to plan, conduct, and administer programs which the Secretary is otherwise authorized to administer (P. L. 93-638, as amended).

    - **31 U.S.C. Chapter 63** provides procedures to be followed in the preparation of Federal contracts, grants, and cooperative agreements.

    - **25 U.S.C. 458(cc)** provides procedures to be followed to establish and implement tribal self-governance compacts.

    - **25 U.S.C. 162a** authorizes the deposit and investment of Indian trust funds.

    - **25 U.S.C. 4001 et seq.** provides procedures to be followed for tribal withdrawal of trust funds, and authorizes the Office of the Special Trustee for American Indians.

    - **25 U.S.C. 459 et seq.** includes numerous provisions affecting specific tribes related to distribution of claims, settlements, and judgments.

2. To remain available until expended

    - **25 U.S.C. 13a** authorizes the carryover of funds, which were not obligated and expended prior to the beginning of the fiscal year succeeding the fiscal year for which such sums were appropriated.

3. That funds for trust management improvements and litigation support may be transferred, as needed, to the Bureau of Indian Affairs ...and to the Departmental Management....

    - **25 U.S.C. 4043(b) (1)** authorizes the Special Trustee to oversee all reform efforts within the Bureau (of Indian Affairs)... and to ensure the establishment of policies, procedures, systems and practices to allow the Secretary to discharge his trust responsibilities in compliance with this chapter. This language also provides the authority for OST to transfer funds to the Office of Hearing and Appeals to address probate backlog reductions as part of trust reform efforts and to the Office of the Solicitor for litigation support.

4. That funds made available to tribes and tribal organizations through contracts or grants obligated during fiscal year 2007, as authorized by the Indian Self-Determination Act of 1975 (25 U.S.C. 450 et seq.), shall remain available until expended by the contractor or grantee:

- **25 U.S.C. 450(l) (c)** authorizes funds obligated for tribal contracts to remain available until expended.

5.   That notwithstanding any other provision of law, the Secretary shall not be required to provide a quarterly statement of performance for any Indian trust account that has not had activity for at least eighteen months and has a balance of $15.00 or less:

- **25 U.S.C. 4043(b)(1)** authorizes the Special Trustee to oversee all reform efforts within the Bureau (of Indian Affairs)... and to ensure the establishment of policies, procedures, systems and practices to allow the Secretary to discharge his/her trust responsibilities in compliance with this chapter.

- **25 U.S.C. 4041 et seq.** requires the reform of trust practices to promote the effective discharge of the Secretary's trust responsibilities.

6.   That the Secretary shall issue an annual account statement and maintain a record of any such accounts and shall permit the balance in each such account to be withdrawn upon the express written request of the account holder.

- **25 U.S.C. 4041 et seq.** requires the reform of trust practices to promote the effective discharge of the Secretary's trust responsibilities.

7.   That not to exceed $50,000 is available for the Secretary to make payments to correct administrative errors of either disbursements from or deposits to Individual Indian Money or tribal accounts after September 30, 2002: Provided further, That erroneous payments that are recovered shall be credited to and remain available in this account for this purpose.

- Interior and Related Agencies Appropriation Act, FY 2002. Annual Appropriations Acts have continued this provision each year since FY 2002.

TAB INSERT

Executive Direction

Activity: Executive Direction
Subactivity: Immediate Office of the Special Trustee

	2013 Full Year CR	2012 Enacted	Fixed Costs & Related Changes (+/-)	Internal Transfers [1] (+/-)	Program Changes (+/-)	2014 Request	Change from 2012 Enacted (+/-)
Executive Direction	*3,315*	**5,046**	**+5**	**-1,160**	**-1,865**	**2,026**	**-3,020**
Executive Direction	*3,315*	*5,046*	*+5*	*-1,160*	*-1,865*	*2,026*	*-3,020*
FTE	*6*	*33*	*0*	*-7*	*-20*	*6*	*-27*

[1] Congress approved $946,000 transfer proposed in August 14, 2012 letter.

Summary of 2014 Program Changes for Executive Direction

Request Component	($000)	FTE
Program Changes:		
Program Reduction and Eliminations	-1,865	-20
TOTAL Program Changes	**-1,865**	**-20**

Justification of 2014 Program Changes

The FY 2014 request for Executive Direction is $2,026,000 and 6 FTE, a program reduction of -$1,865,000 from the 2012 Enacted level and a reduction of -20 FTE from the FY 2012 actual FTE count.

Internal transfers include:
- -$973,000 and 6 FTE to Field Operations for the Investments group. Congress approved $946,000 transfer proposed in August 14, 2012 letter.
- -$187,000 and 1 FTE to External Affairs

Program Reductions and Eliminations (-$1,865,000/-20 FTE) - Executive Direction's program change of -$1,865,000 is the result of the elimination of the National Indian Program Training Center contract in the amount of -$727,000, a reduction to Trust Regulations, Policies, and Procedures of -$1,314,000, and the elimination of the Product Development Initiative of -$231,000. OST programs will create, modify or eliminate regulations, policies and procedures working with the Assistant Secretary – Indian Affairs' Policies and Regulations Group, the Department, and the Solicitor's Office.

Program Overview

Executive Direction ($2,026,000/ 6 FTE) - The Special Trustee is charged with general oversight of Indian trust asset reform efforts Department-wide to ensure proper and efficient discharge of the Secretary's fiduciary trust responsibilities to federally recognized Indian Tribes, Alaska Natives, and individual Indians. OST was created to ensure that the Department establishes appropriate policies and procedures, develops necessary systems, and

> OST supports legislative proposals addressing needed technical corrections and administrative improvements for implementing trust reform, which will continue to improve services to Indian trust beneficiaries.

takes affirmative actions to reform the management of Indian trust funds. In carrying out the management and oversight of Indian trust funds, the Secretary has a responsibility to ensure that trust accounts are properly maintained, invested, and reported in accordance with the *American Indian Trust Fund Management Reform Act of 1994*, Congressional action, and other applicable laws. Funds provided for OST directly contribute to the appropriate oversight needed to further the Department's Indian Fiduciary Trust Responsibilities.

Executive leadership and guidance provided by the immediate office effects performance at all levels of OST, including the delivery of beneficiary services, promoting tribal self-governance and self-determination, managing financial trust assets and monitoring all efforts to reform and improve the manner in which the Department conducts its Indian fiduciary trust responsibilities. In addition, OST continues to promote better integration of budget and performance, develop a workforce plan that ensures a skilled workforce now and in the future, and properly account for financial resources.

2014 Program Performance

- Support the Secretarial Commission on Indian Trust Administration and Reform established by Secretarial Order 3292, including working with the Commission's management consultant to complete its Department-wide assessment of the Trust Administration System.
- Provide oversight, guidance, and implementation of reform activities.
- Provide direction for special projects, programs, and highly sensitive issue areas of Congressional, Departmental, OMB, or Secretarial concern.
- Oversee trust activities throughout the Department – program managers are expected to advise the Office on a number of complex and sensitive issues relating to organization, reengineering, ongoing litigation and other trust activities.
- Support the work of the Special Trustee's Advisory Board.
- Create informed partnerships with other bureau and office directors in the Department to achieve positive trust reform outcomes.
- Provide leadership in the implementation of all aspects of the Individual Indian Money Account Litigation Settlement

TAB INSERT

Program Operations

Activity: Program Operations and Support
Subactivity: Field Operations

	2013 Full Year CR	2012 Enacted	Fixed Costs & Related Changes (+/-)	Internal Transfers (+/-)	Program Changes (+/-)	2014 Request	Change from 2012 Enacted (+/-)
Program Operations							
Field Operations	26,278	23,433	+198	+973	+143	24,747	+1,314
Total	**26,278**	**23,433**	**+198**	**973**	**143**	**24,747**	**1,314**
FTE	*220*	*206*	*+0*	*+6*	*+5*	*217*	*+11*

Summary of 2014 Program Changes for Field Operations

Request Component	($000)	FTE
Program Changes:		
Increase for program operations	+143	+5
TOTAL Program Changes	**+143**	**5**

Justification of 2014 Program Changes

The FY 2014 budget request for Field Operations is $24,747,000 and 217 FTE, a program change of +$143,000 from the FY 2012 Enacted budget level. The FY 2012 FTE is actual and reflects lapses due to attrition.   As part of OST's realignment, the Investments group was returned to Program Operations beginning in FY 2013, as reflected by the internal transfer of $973,000 and 6 FTE. Congress approved $946,000 transfer proposed in August 14, 2012 letter.

Program Enhancements (+$143,000/+5 FTE) - Additional funding is requested to address the increased workload resulting from the Individual Indian Money Account Litigation Settlement and the increase in FTE reflects the planned staffing level needed to meet the workload requirements.

Program Overview
Field Operations ($24,747,000/217 FTE) - Field Operations is the primary point of contact for trust beneficiaries (Tribes, individual Indians, and Alaska Natives) seeking information and services in conjunction with their trust assets. The field staff assists beneficiaries on a daily basis at regional, agency, and urban locations regarding account statements, account balances, account updates, receipts, disbursements, probate processing, leases, and leasing. Other trust asset information important to beneficiaries, such as statutory or regulatory changes affecting trust asset management, is also provided.

Field Operations plays a key role in leading the Department's outreach efforts to beneficiaries. Outreach events include staff attendance at community meetings and pow-wows with a focus on providing information on asset management and trust reform initiatives, as well as holding financial skills training for Individual Indian Money (IIM) beneficiaries throughout Indian Country. As a result of implementation of the Individual Indian Money Account Litigation Settlement, Field Operations will also provide outreach support to promote understanding of the Land Buy-Back Program's purpose in acquiring fractional interests in trust or restricted lands.

Regional Trust Administrators (RTAs) and Fiduciary Trust Officers (FTOs) in selected locations provide the managerial presence for responsive and proactive beneficiary services at the local level in cooperation and collaboration with BIA and other Departmental Agencies engaged in Indian trust matters. Beneficiary accounts for whom OST does not have a current address are referred to as "Whereabouts Unknown" (WAU) account holders. In FY 2013 OST received $35 million in trust from Individual Indian Money Account Litigation Settlement Stage I payments for WAU account holders, and an additional $21 million for supervised accounts. To facilitate disbursement of these funds, Field Operations is significantly increasing its outreach efforts to locate WAU account holders. With the Stage II payments anticipated in the beginning of FY 2014, OST will receive similar amounts into trust and Field Operations will face another surge requiring increased efforts to locate missing beneficiaries.

RTAs provide technical assistance on trust matters, supporting the Department of the Interior in meeting its fiduciary obligations to individual Indians, Alaska Natives, and Tribes. This assistance includes responding to complex Congressional, Tribal, and individual beneficiary inquiries; monitoring statutory and regulatory developments; and providing risk management and litigation support activities. RTAs provide direct line authority and supervision to 45 agency level FTOs. In addition, they are responsible for reviewing and authorizing complex and high dollar trust transactions.

Fiduciary Trust Officer and staff conducting beneficiary outreach.

The FTOs are located across Indian Country and in select urban locations with significant trust beneficiary populations. This local presence allows beneficiaries easy, direct access to individuals dedicated to meeting their trust needs. FTOs and support staff provide beneficiaries with convenient access to trust account information and other trust products and services. FTOs, like the RTAs, are delegated with disbursement approval authority and oversight responsibility. The goal is to provide services to beneficiaries that are trusted, timely, accurate, and responsive to their needs. FTO responsibilities include coordinating trust asset management activities with the BIA and other related government agencies in their respective geographic area. FTOs provide guidance to support staff in the examination, verification, and management of accounts and accounting information. They also ensure that responses to trust beneficiary requests are tracked and addressed courteously and accurately. The FTOs' activities and beneficiary focus significantly enhance the Department's ability to meet its trust obligations to individual Indians, Alaska Natives, and Tribes.

The Trust Beneficiary Call Center (TBCC), located in Albuquerque, New Mexico, is a nationwide toll free call center (1-888-678-6836) that provides convenient "one-stop" service for beneficiary inquiries. The call center's operating hours are 7 00 AM to 6:00 PM MT Monday through Friday and 8:00 AM to

Noon MT on Saturday. Beneficiaries can easily access information and assistance regarding their account statements, account balances, other account attributes, receipts, disbursements, leases, probate processing, and other trust activities, including reform developments and implementation (e.g., leasing, lockbox, oil and gas activity, and debit card) at their convenience by calling the toll free number. In addition, beneficiaries may request a disbursement from or an update to their IIM account. The TBCC also responds to written beneficiary requests. In an effort to reduce the number of WAU account holders, the TBCC staff handles and processes all OST mailings and delivery failures through the Return Mail Project. The TBCC also implemented a tracking and case management tool for the BIA Social Services Program to improve communication and collaborative efforts between OST and BIA for the management of supervised accounts. Contract personnel trained on various trust beneficiary issues and with access to all trust systems make up the majority of TBCC staff. Field Operations monitors the contractor's work and provides technical direction, guidance and managerial direction as needed.

After eight years of operation, the call center has received over 1.1 million calls and provided first-line resolution in excess of 95 percent of call requests. First-line resolution by TBCC means that the call center is able to address the beneficiary's inquiry without referring the caller to the field offices for assistance. This level of first-line resolution is substantially higher than the industry average of 49 percent for government and non-profit organizations and allows BIA and OST field staff to focus on other trust duties. Occasionally, the complexity of a beneficiary's inquiry requires OST staff to obtain information from other agencies in the Department of the Interior that may require extensive research.

During the period of Individual Indian Money Account Litigation Settlement Stage I payments, the TBCC received an additional 10,500 calls. It is anticipated that Stage II disbursements will result in a similar increase in beneficiary inquiries. Historical trend analysis suggests that, depending upon the role of the TBCC in the Land Buy-Back program, the TBCC will receive between 200,000 to 216,000 inquiries for FY 2013.

In the first two quarters of FY 2013, 13,500 WAU account holders were identified, their addresses updated, and $13.5 million was disbursed to these beneficiaries. The combination of increased call volume and updating of account holder records significantly increased Field Operations' workload. During FY 2012, Field Operations located approximately 18,800 WAU accountholders with total account balances in excess of $21.4 million. At the end of FY 2012, there were 85,374 WAU beneficiaries representing $67.2 million.

The Field Operations Service Center tracking system is utilized by all field staff to track requests, avoid duplication, and assure that beneficiaries receive consistent responses and information. In FY 2013, the TBCC tracking system will continue to be used to develop paperless automated beneficiary accounting transactions, thus eliminating manual processing and streamlining the processes. In FY 2014 Field Operations anticipates a conversion to a new automated program (Service Manager) that will require remapping of all existing data fields and forms, to accommodate the new version and interface with the current Service Center databases.

In FY 2013, the Office of Trust Fund Investments (OTFI) was transferred from Trust Services to Field Operations. OTFI manages in-house approximately 2,000 separate tribal investment portfolios and the IMM Fund portfolio which has more than 300,000 individual account holders.
OTFI also continues to offer expert investment services to the U.S. Treasury for other trust fund accounts pursuant to duly executed MOUs.

2014 Program Performance

In FY 2014, Field Operations will meet its fiduciary obligations to individual Indians, Alaska Natives, and Tribes by providing beneficiaries with a dedicated primary point of contact focused on providing beneficiary services in a timely, courteous, and accurate manner. Specifically, Field Operations will take the following actions:

- Support implementation of the Individual Indian Money Account Litigation Settlement payout process by locating WAU account holders.
- Maintain and enhance strategic partnerships with the Department's bureaus and offices with Indian trust responsibilities. These partnerships enhance communication with beneficiaries and promote a beneficiary focus throughout the Department.
- Continue interaction with tribal, individual Indian, and Alaska Native beneficiaries through local community outreach programs focused on asset management and trust reform initiatives. Community outreach informs beneficiaries of current trust initiatives and services available to them. It also provides Field Operations, as the primary point of beneficiary contact, with an additional channel of communication to reach beneficiaries who might not otherwise be in contact with the Department. These outreach events are usually in partnership with other agencies or organizations that can assist beneficiaries by providing information or services relevant to the management of individual and tribal trust assets.
- Continued interactions with tribal leaders to discuss investment of tribal trust funds (including investment training), land management and other issues important to the Tribes and their communities.
- Continue interactions with Indian organizations to promote and support trust initiatives.
- Continue to participate in the implementation and continuation of reform initiatives with BIA and other government entities. The participation of Field Operations in trust reform initiatives ensures that these efforts are effective at the local level.
- Proactively identify and assist in the implementation of additional reform activities as needed, in support of ever-evolving program areas such as trust program training, developing policies and procedures, streamlining business processes, risk, and records management. As the primary point of beneficiary contact, Field Operations is uniquely situated to identify and respond to evolving beneficiary needs.
- Provide financial skills training to IIM beneficiaries throughout Indian Country as an integral part of its community outreach activities. This training uses culturally sensitive techniques and methods geared to Native American audiences. Topics include balancing checkbooks, applying for credit, reading a credit application, budgeting, investing, and planning for the future. There will be a special effort to offer this training to minors approaching the age of majority through the deployment of an

online curriculum. Minors will learn to handle income to build financial stability. The training will also help elders with the special challenge of managing resources they may consider leaving to their heirs.

- Respond to 90 percent of beneficiary inquiries within two business days and respond to the balance of these inquiries within 30 days.

- Actively support self-determination efforts by engaging Tribal and individual Indian beneficiaries in the management of their trust assets.

- Continue to advocate establishing direct deposit or debit card capabilities for individual Indian and Alaska Native beneficiaries and electronic fund transfers for tribal governments. Direct deposit and debit cards provide faster disbursement while reducing the risk of lost or stolen funds.

- Continue to work with tribal leadership to stress the importance of proper estate planning and continue partnerships with local bar associations, legal services organizations, and law schools to advocate the importance of estate planning for individual Indian beneficiaries. These working relationships are at no or minimal cost to the beneficiary in response to the Department's policy of no longer providing will drafting assistance to owners of trust interests. Proper estate planning can reduce fractionation and enhance the use and value of trust lands for beneficiaries while reducing long term administrative costs to the Department. The relationships established by Field Operations provide a valuable service to beneficiaries and will support the Land Buy-Back program's objectives of reducing land fractionation.

- Maintain Fiduciary Trust Officer presence in field offices.

- Address Field Operations recommendations from internal and external program reviews.

- Continue to improve the efficiencies of the lockbox operations.

- Continue the migration of trust transaction activities to the local level, reducing redundancy and improving upon efficiencies.

- Continue automation to improve processes and processing timeframe, allowing Agency staff to respond to beneficiary inquiries.

- Explore automated call-tree options within TBCC.

- Work with the Secretarial Commission on Indian Trust Administration and Reform to improve trust services to Indian Country.

- Promote the use of electronic access to account information through the Strata Web product. Eighty-five Tribes are using this product, which allows Tribes to access their trust account information on an as needed basis through a web based product to support Tribal self-determination. On March 6, 2013 a pilot was launched offering Strata Web account access to individual users. Field Operation's goal is to offer this service to thousands of other individual accountholders.

Activity: Program Operations and Support
Subactivity: Appraisal Services

	2013 Full Year CR	2012 Enacted	Fixed Costs & Related Changes (+/-)	Internal Transfers (+/-)	Program Changes (+/-)	2014 Request	Change from 2012 Enacted (+/-)
Program Operations							
Appraisal Services	10,755	10,691	+64	+0	-11	10,744	+53
Total	**10,755**	**10,691**	**+64**	**0**	**-11**	**10,744**	**53**
FTE	*71*	*68*	*+0*	*+0*	*3*	*71*	*3*

Summary of 2014 Program Changes for Appraisal Services

Request Component	($000)	FTE
Program Changes:		
Savings due to efficiencies.	-11	+3
TOTAL Program Changes	**-11**	**+3**

Justification of 2014 Program Changes

The FY 2014 budget request for the Appraisal Services program is $10,744,000 and 71 FTE, a program reduction of -$11,000 from the FY 2012 Enacted.

Savings due to efficiencies (-$11,000/+3FTE) – The reduction in funding for Appraisal Services is a result of improved efficiencies by streamlining the appraisal process. The FY 2012 FTE count is actual FTE, and includes lapses due to attrition; the +3 FTE reflects the planned staffing level of 71, as in prior years.

Program Overview

Appraisal Services ($10,744,000/71 FTE) - The Office of Appraisal Services (OAS) is responsible for the Indian lands valuation program, which was established to provide impartial estimates of opinions of value for a specific type of real property interests held or owned in trust or restricted status for Indian Tribes, individual Indians, and Alaska Natives. The types of land transactions include, but are not limited to, sales, leases, rights-of-way; exchanges; grazing permits and trespass settlements, as well as other types of real estate transactions.

OAS consists of state certified general appraisers who provide the valuations in accordance with nationally recognized appraisal standards and methods and techniques. Valuations are also completed in compliance with DOI and OAS appraisal policies and procedures.

It is DOI's policy that all appraisal practices completed by OAS conform to the current Uniform Standards of Professional Appraisal Practice (USPAP) promulgated by the Appraisal Standards Board of The Appraisal Foundation—updated and published regularly—and the current edition of the Uniform Appraisal Standards for Federal Land Acquisitions (UASFLA) promulgated by the Interagency Land Acquisition Conference, as applicable.

In FY 2014, OAS's foremost priority will be to support self-determination and self-governance contracts/compacts by providing quality appraisals of Indian land. OAS will enter into a reimbursable agreement with the Land Buy-Back office to perform all appraisals in conjunction with the Land Buy-Back program.

> OAS continues to address appraisal requests on trust lands. OAS completed *6,575* appraisals in FY 2012 (excluding appraisals completed using the Mass Appraisal Valuations System (MAVS), which is an automated valuation system) and anticipates completing approximately 6,500 appraisals in FY 2013 (again, excluding any appraisals completed using MAVS). OAS also anticipates continuing efforts to include information from compact/contract Tribes on appraisals completed to maintain a comprehensive database on appraisal workload throughout Indian Country. In 2012, the Office of Appraisal Services Information System (OASIS) was implemented in OAS as well as several BIA Regions and Agencies. The Mass Appraisal Program System (MAPS) has also been implemented in some OAS regions to improve productivity and provide more efficiency within the appraisal program.

2014 Program Performance

- Complete 85 percent of appraisal requests received from the client within requestor business requirements.
- Continue to improve and streamline the appraisal business process, which includes the use of Office of Appraisal Services Information System (OASIS), an automated appraisal request tracking system developed by OAS and joint implemented by OAS and OST Information Resources. The application allows for improved transparency, streamlining of BIA agency/tribal request interactions and standardizing of appraisal requests.
- Continue to reduce the time and cost to complete appraisals by conducting 20 percent of current appraisal requests using OAS staff.
- Continue to assist/support the Land Buy-Back Program in streamlining the appraisal process, to include providing OASIS for tracking appraisals, uploading appraisal information to the Trust Asset and Accounting Management System (TAAMS), Geographic Information System (GIS) for mapping, and using the Mass Appraisal Program System as a template for appraisals; sharing sales data between OAS Field Operations and the Land Buy-Back Program Division.
- Continue the deployment of appraisal applications software to manage comparable market data and generate appraisals compliant with USPAP and UASFLA, where applicable.
- Update and implement OAS appraisal program policies, procedures, and guidance to streamline operations and establish consistency.

Activity: Program Operations and Support
Subactivity: Trust Services

	2013 Full Year CR	2012 Enacted	Fixed Costs & Related Changes (+/-)	Internal Transfers (+/-)	Program Changes (+/-)	2014 Request	Change from 2012 Enacted (+/-)
Program Operations							
Trust Services	*28,690*	26,715	+112	+2,326	-207	28,946	+2,231
Total	**28,690**	**26,715**	**+112**	**2,326**	**-207**	**28,946**	**2,231**
FTE	*124*	*119*	*+0*	*+5*	*0*	*124*	*5*

Summary of 2014 Program Changes for Trust Services

Request Component	($000)	FTE
Program Changes:		
Elimination of internship program.	-207	+0
TOTAL Program Changes	**-207**	**+0**

Justification of 2014 Program Changes

The 2014 budget request for Trust Services is $28,946,000 and 124 FTE, a net program change of -$207,000 from the FY 2012 Enacted level. Internal transfers include $2,326,000 and +5 FTE, for the Data Quality and Integrity program.

Elimination of Internship Program (-207,000/0 FTE) - The proposed funding for Trust Services includes a decrease of -$207,000, primarily for the elimination of the Internship Program ($142,000) and as a result of improved efficiencies through the development of an application program that reduces manual entry requirements. As part of the OST's realignment in FY 2013, Trust Services will absorb the Data Quality and Integrity program, as reflected by an internal transfer of +$2,326,000 from Trust Accountability.

Program Overview

Trust Services ($28,946,000/124 FTE) - The Congress has designated the Secretary of the Interior as the trustee delegate with responsibility for the monetary and non-monetary resources held in trust on behalf of American Indian Tribes, individual Indians, and other trust funds. In carrying out the management and oversight of the Indian trust funds, the Secretary has a fiduciary responsibility to ensure that trust accounts are properly maintained, invested, and reported in accordance with the Reform Act, Congressional action, and other applicable laws.

Trust Services is responsible for the individual Indian, Alaska Native and tribal trust funds accounting, investment and reporting fiduciary responsibilities of the Department. This Office provides leadership, guidance and oversight of the development of policies, procedures, and processes to ensure proper management of trust funds on behalf of beneficiaries. Trust Services supports Indian Fiduciary Trust Responsibilities through performance measures of providing timely and accurate financial account information to trust beneficiaries, the timely recording of oil and gas royalties in the trust accounting system and the accurate processing of financial information in trust beneficiary accounts.

> Trust Services is currently using metric performance data to assess the efficiency and effectiveness of trust operations as exhibited by:
>
> - Assist in the promotion of debit cards and electronic funds transfer to reduce the cost of disbursing funds via paper check to beneficiaries.
>
> - Phase out of certain personnel services by using increased automation and insourcing the remaining functions.
>
> - Utilizing employee performance metrics to assess and validate individual and team performance. Data is used to identify performance standards and training needs.
>
> - Establishing, revising, and monitoring workload and processing timeframes.

Trust Services manages nearly over $4.4 billion in funds held in trust for federally recognized Indian Tribes, individual Indian, and Alaska Native beneficiaries. Approximately $3.7 billion is held in about 3,000 tribal and other trust fund accounts, including the Alaska Native Escrow Fund. Approximately $700 million is held on behalf of individual Indians in about 387,000 beneficiary accounts. The balances that have accumulated in the Tribal trust have resulted from claims and judgment awards, investment income, and revenues from approximately 55 million acres of trust lands. Revenues are derived from subsurface mineral extractions (coal, oil, gas, and uranium) timber, grazing, and other surface leases. Individual Indian Money (IIM) balances are generally on deposit as a result of restricted accounts (e.g., minors, estates, Whereabouts Unknown).

The program's business objectives are to manage and invest fund assets to provide beneficial rates of return; and to timely and accurately collect, disburse, and account for funds associated with trust assets. Accomplishment of these objectives enables the Department to provide accurate and timely information to trust beneficiaries. The accuracy and timeliness of information is comprised of several factors: timely processing and posting of cash, account maintenance, and investment income transactions. Reconciliation and activity reporting on trust accounts impacts accuracy and timely reporting to beneficiaries.

Trust Services is responsible for reconciling subsidiary and control accounts and monitoring trust funds activities. This office prepares internal and external financial accounting reports for trust funds. It also is responsible for the accurate and timely preparation and submission of appropriate external reports and required tax forms. The reconciliation of trust fund activities include custodial management of proprietary data, compliance and interface with Treasury cash flow reports, and the receipting of funds from BIA and the Office of Natural Resources Revenue (ONRR).

Trust Funds Accounting System (TFAS) – To comply with
the provisions of the Reform Act, (P. L. 103-412, title IV,
Sec. 401, Oct. 25, 1994, 108 Stat. 4249), OST uses the
TFAS, a commercial off-the-shelf system owned and
operated by a third party vendor. The existing contract was
awarded during FY 2008. Some of the costs associated with
the TFAS contract are based upon the number of accounts
on the system (open and closed). Currently, TFAS has over
387,000 open and approximately 15,000 closed accounts.
Of the 387,000 open accounts approximately 97,000 were
non-income accounts. A Statement of Performance is
produced in TFAS for non-income accounts, which includes
real property assets. In addition to normal processing, items
included in the core price are the daily pricing of securities;

Check processing machine.

software licenses that allow Tribes access via the Internet using Strata Web; software licenses, security,
custody, and investment settlement services.

Estimated TFAS Total Accounts				
Status	**2011 Actual**	**2012 Actual**	**2013 Estimate**	**2014 Estimate**
Open $$$ and Land	204,470	209,134	200,000	200,000
Open Land only	94,981	96,589	95,000	80,000
Open $$$ only	84,144	81,414	70,000	80,000
Closed*	14,054	15,222	15,000	30,000
TOTAL	**397,649**	**402,359**	**380,000**	**390,000**

** Accounts that are coded as closed for more than 18 months are periodically removed from the
system. There will always be some closed accounts on the system. Also, as a result of the
Individual Indian Money Account Litigation Settlement Land Buy-Back Program, additional
accounts are anticipated to be closed in FY 2014.*

Within Trust Services, the Data Quality and Integrity (DQ&I) program funds a trust data cleanup project
where TAAMS Critical Data Elements (CDE) are validated and/or corrected and Post-QA reviews of
TAAMS system entries are conducted to help ensure updates to CDE are accurate. From FY 2007
through FY 2010, the DQ&I project supported BIA's effort to convert to the TAAMS Leasing module
and to guide and assist with BIA's TAAMS document encoding backlog efforts. This was accomplished
by: 1) assisting the BIA with their encumbrance and conveyance document encoding into TAAMS; 2)
correcting multiple landowner identification (ID) numbers; and 3) analyzing landowner ID numbers and
ownership interests in the TAAMS Title module to determine their accuracy. DQ&I also continued to
perform Post-QA reviews of document encoding entries made into TAAMS. It is anticipated that the
Post-QA review process will be ongoing indefinitely to help ensure that TAAMS CDE remain accurate.

In FY 2014, DQ&I in collaboration with BIA will: 1) assist with trust document encoding backlogs; 2)
assist with land title research and correction, 3) lead trust data clean-up tasks that may arise as a result of
risk assessments, and 4) continue performing Post-QA review of TAAMS entries.

In FY 2014 Trust Services top priority will continue to be the management of Tribal and Individual Indian Money funds through the accurate and timely execution of investment, disbursement, receipt, accounting, and reporting functions.

2014 Program Performance

The FY 2014 funding allows Trust Services to:

- Attain at least 99 percent accuracy for financial information initially processed in trust beneficiary accounts.
- Record at least 99 percent of ONRR royalty revenue within 24 hours of receipt.
- Maintain necessary Tribal trust litigation support.
- Continue to process up to 10,000 probate orders and distribution of funds to beneficiaries.
- Continue to process over one million account maintenance transactions annually.
- Continue reconciliation and clean-up of suspense and special deposit accounts.
- Continue to process over two billion dollars in receipts and disbursements annually.
- Continue daily reconciliation of all trust funds receipts/disbursements with Treasury (over 8.8 million transactions annually).
- Continue to compile monthly and annual financial statements, applicable tax reports, and required regulatory financial reports.

Activity: Program Operations and Support
Subactivity: Historical Trust Accounting

	2013 Full Year CR	2012 Enacted	Fixed Costs & Related Changes (+/-)	Internal Transfers (+/-)	Program Changes (+/-)	2014 Request	Change from 2012 Enacted (+/-)
Program Operations							
Historical Trust Accounting	*31,121*	31,121	+18	-1,108	-6,986	23,045	-8,076
Total	*31,121*	**31,121**	**+18**	**-1,108**	**-6,986**	**23,045**	**-8,076**
FTE	*20*	*19*	*+0*	*+0*	*1*	*20*	*1*

Summary of 2014 Program Changes for Program Operations

Request Component	($000)	FTE
Program Changes:		
Reduction in contracts	-6,986	+1
TOTAL Program Changes	**-6,986**	**+1**

Justification of 2014 Program Changes
The FY 2014 budget request for the Office of Historical Trust Accounting (OHTA) is $23,045,000 and 20 FTE, a net program change of -$6,986,000 from the FY 2012 enacted budget. The FY 2012 FTE number is actual FTE and reflects lapses due to attrition; the additional +1 FTE for FY 2014 reflects the staffing level without lapses.

Reduction in Contract Services (-$6,986,000/+1 FTE) - In FY 2014, a program change of -$6,986,000 is proposed for OHTA. To achieve this reduction OHTA has consolidated space and will implement reductions in contractor assistance. These reductions and planned program performance are based partly on the premise that the Federal government and other parties use readily available data and proceed to settlement. If current settlements do not come to fruition, trial preparation becomes necessary, and/or Individual Indian Money (IIM) litigation requires further document research, document production or research for accounts that have opted out of the Individual Indian Money Account Litigation Settlement, Interior will have to reassess its strategy to meet these additional requirements. The FY 2012 FTE count is actual FTE, and includes lapses due to attrition; the +1 FTE reflects the planned staffing level of 20, as in prior years.

Program Overview

Office of Historical Trust Accounting ($23,045,000/20 FTE) - In July 2001, the Office of Historical Trust Accounting (OHTA) was created by Secretarial Order to plan, organize, direct, and execute the historical accounting of Individual Indian Money (IIM) accounts (OHTA's responsibilities were later expanded to include the provision of historical accounts for tribal accounts). OHTA's management model is based on a small staff of Federal employees directing the efforts of a number of individual contractors. The contractors have provided critical technical expertise in areas such as accounting services, historical research, information resources, data security, statistical analysis, document search, collection, and reproduction.

The Department and OHTA are involved in lawsuits filed by or on behalf of 66 Tribes. These cases are in various Federal District Courts and the Court of Federal Claims. OHTA is continuing its strategy of satisfying the critical information needs of the litigating Tribes through document production and organization, digitization, and analysis of tribal accounts. OHTA also will continue to support active litigation and settlement negotiations working with Department of Justice (DOJ) and DOI Office of the Solicitor (SOL).

OHTA anticipates the more Tribes will file tribal trust claims against the Federal government, as some Tribes were not previously aware of the option to do so. OHTA also is providing data, analysis, and other support necessary to implement the Claims Resolution Act of 2010, which authorized settlement of the *Cobell v. Salazar* class action litigation.

2014 Program Performance

In FY 2014, OHTA's priority will continue to be historical analysis, research, and support for tribal trust litigation and settlement efforts.

Tribal Historical Accounting ($17,600,000) - OHTA will continue to compile, analyze, and explain an extensive volume of documents and data concerning how the Federal Government managed various funds held in trust for Native American tribes in order to settle or defend the tribal litigation.

As with prior years, OHTA's efforts will focus on helping achieve negotiated settlements of tribal trust fund accounting and related claims. In addition, OHTA will continue to provide technical and factual support to DOJ and SOL for those cases where negotiated settlement is not possible and the parties are proceeding to trial. More specifically, OHTA anticipates that its activities in support of negotiated settlement and/or defense of litigation proceeding to trial will include: informational briefings about trust fund accounts and data; document search, imaging, and coding; compilation, validation, and maintenance of trust account databases; settlement calculations and analysis; account and/or transaction mapping, analysis, and reconciliation; investment performance analysis and reporting; fact and expert testimony; response to tribal discovery requests and questions; and preparation and presentation of account lists, account statements, technical exhibits, and demonstrative aids.

Special Deposit Accounts/Youpee ($3,628,000) - OHTA will continue to research the rightful owners of historical residual balances in special deposit accounts and seek to distribute $250,000 to individual Indians, Tribes, and third parties. This funding also will be used to perform the research and analysis necessary to distribute trust funds residing in Youpee Escheat Accounts. The latter reflect income from land interests that has escheated (transferred) to Tribes under legislation that the Supreme Court deemed unconstitutional.

IIM Historical Accounting ($1,817,000) - OHTA expects that all of the Stage II distributions of the Individual Indian Money Account Litigation Settlement will have been completed by the end of FY 2014. In FY 2014, various tasks and work may be necessary to implement the Claims Resolution Act and the Individual Indian Money Account Litigation Settlement, including resolution of disputed distributions, new claims arising from possible class members, and claims of individual Indians who have opted-out of the Trust Asset Mismanagement class.

Activity: Program Operations and Support
Subactivity: Trust Accountability

	2013 Full Year CR	2012 Enacted	Fixed Costs & Related Changes (+/-)	Internal Transfers (+/-)	Program Changes (+/-)	2014 Request	Change from 2012 Enacted (+/-)
Program Operations							
Trust Accountability	0	15,511	+0	-11,679	-3,832	0	-15,511
Total	**0**	**15,511**	**+0**	**-11,679**	**-3,832**	**0**	**-15,511**
FTE	*0*	*13*	*+0*	*-10*	*-3*	*0*	*-13*

Summary of 2014 Program Changes for Trust Accountability

Request Component	($000)	FTE
Program Changes:		
Program Completion.	-3,832	-3
TOTAL Program Changes	**-3,832**	**-3**

Justification of 2014 Program Changes

The FY 2014 budget request for Trust Accountability is $0 and 0 FTE, a program change of -$3,832,000 and -3 FTE from the 2012 Enacted.

Internal transfers include 10 FTE and:

- -$8,716,000 to Budget, Finance and Administration for the Office of Hearings and Appeals
- -$637,000 to Trust Review Audit for the Risk Management program
- -$2,326,000 to Trust Services for Data Quality and Integrity program

Program Completion (-$3,832/-3 FTE) - As certain trust reform projects were completed, on-going functions and personnel resources were realigned into other OST offices. Trust training ($1.8M), and product development ($1M) were eliminated. As a result of the consolidation of probate offices, and savings from the digitization of its probate records, funding for the Office of Hearings and Appeals was reduced by $1.0 million, resulting in the elimination of the Trust Accountability division.

THIS PAGE INTENTIONALLY LEFT BLANK

TAB INSERT

Program Support

Activity: Program Operations and Support
Subactivity: Program Support

	2013 Full Year CR	2012 Enacted	Fixed Costs & Related Changes (+/-)	Internal Transfers (+/-)	Program Changes (+/-)	2014 Request	Change from 2012 Enacted (+/-)
Program Support	52,847	39,558	-1,790	10,648	+1,753	50,169	10,611
Business Management	39,990	21,939	-1,884	+14,454	+197	34,706	12,767
Program Management	12,857	17,619	+94	-3,806	+1,556	15,463	-2,156
FTE	197	181	+0	+13	+6	200	19

Overview of Program Support

Business Management and Program Management comprise the subactivity of Program Support. Although the programs focus on different specialized aspects of OST, both support fiduciary trust responsibilities to tribal and individual Indian beneficiaries.

Business Management provides strategic planning, workforce planning, training design for staff development, and the execution of special projects as directed by Executive management. Various administrative functions, budget services, information resources, interface with external organizations, litigation coordination, and clerical support, are also provided by Business Management.

Program Management provides independent audits of Indian fiduciary trust programs and monitors implementation of corrective actions to address any deficiencies. Independent from Trust Review and Audit, the Risk Management group conducts a comprehensive program to identify and mitigate risk. Management and operation of the American Indian Records Repository also falls within Program Management. Tangent to the management of records, the program is responsible for the development of records management policies, and provides records management training and support services to OST and Indian Affairs.

Activity: Program Operations and Support
Subactivity: Program Support – Business Management

	2013 Full Year CR	2012 Enacted	Fixed Costs & Related Changes (+/-)	Internal Transfers (+/-)	Program Changes (+/-)	2014 Request	Change from 2012 Enacted (+/-)
Business Management	*39,990*	**21,939**	**-1,884**	**+14,454**	**+197**	**34,706**	**+12,767**
Business Management	*1,872*	0	+16	+1,565	+291	1,872	+1,872
Budget, Finance & Administration	*29,921*	14,140	-1,939	+12,352	+62	24,615	+10,475
Litigation Support	*[3,986]*	*[3,986]*	+0	+0	+0	*[3,986]*	+0
Office of Hearings and Appeals	*[9,713]*	*[9,713]*	+0	[-997]	+0	*[8,716]*	*[-997]*
Information Resources	*6,768*	6,378	+31	+0	+190	6,599	+221
Office of External Affairs	*1,429*	1,421	+8	+537	-346	1,620	+199
FTE	*87*	*72*	*+0*	*+13*	*+3*	*88*	*16*

Summary of 2014 Program Changes for Program Support - Business Management

Request Component	($000)	FTE
Program Changes:		
Expanded Operational workload.	+353	+3
Increase for program enhancement.	+190	+0
Elimination of Inter-Tribal Monitoring Association grant.	-346	+0
TOTAL Program Changes	**+197**	**+3**

Justification of 2014 Program Changes

The FY 2014 budget request for Program Support – Business Management is $34,706,000 and 88 FTE, a net program change of +$197,000 and +3 FTE from the 2012 Enacted.

Expanded Operation Workload (+$353,000/+3 FTE) - OST's realignment included the creation of a Deputy Special Trustee position to head the entire Business Management division and resulted in an expanded workload within the Business Management Group and the Office of Budget, Finance, and Administration.

IT Transformation (+190,000) – This increase covers certain up-front costs related to the Departmental IT Transformation initiative.

Elimination of Inter-Tribal Monitoring Association Grant (-$346,000) – The purpose of the grant to ITMA is completed and the grant will not continue into 2014.

Internal Transfers:

- Business Management will have an internal transfer of $1,565,000 representing the transfer of 12 staff from Executive Direction as part of OST's realignment.
- Budget, Finance and Administration (BF&A) will have internal transfers of +$3,986,474 from the Office of Trust Records for Litigation Support, +$8,716,000 from Trust Accountability for the Office of Hearings and Appeals, and -$350,000 to External Affairs for a net internal transfer totaling $12,352,000.
- External Affairs will receive an internal transfer of +$187,282 from Executive Direction for one position in addition to the incoming internal transfer of +$350,000, for a net internal transfer totaling +$537.

Program Overview

The offices encompassing Business Management provide the critical infrastructure and administrative services that enable the organization to function as an effective fiduciary trustee. It also provides modern, appropriate systems and tools to manage the fiduciary trust responsibilities. Program elements include Business Management, Office of Information Resources (IR), Office of Budget, Finance, and Administration (BF&A), and the Office of External Affairs (OEA).

Business Management ($1,872,000/14 FTE) - Business Management includes the Deputy Special Trustee for Business Management, a litigation coordination team, and a support staff that provide a variety of services to the entire OST organization. The litigation coordination team serves as liaison, and in an advisory capacity, for Indian trust litigation issues and related matters, representing OST at meetings, presentations, and in other public forums with Departmental offices, plaintiff attorneys and general public. This group frequently defines OST positions by providing sound quantitative evidence and analysis. The litigation coordination team develops and implements specific litigation related goals and objectives, as well as researching, compiling, and reviewing documents relevant to cash management and investment practices.

Other vital support functions provided by the Business Management program include strategic planning, workforce planning, training design for staff development, and the execution of special projects as directed by Executive management. The program also provides administrative and clerical support to Executive management.

Budget, Finance and Administration ($24,615,000/31 FTE) - The BF&A office supports OST in carrying out its fiduciary trust responsibilities to federally recognized American Indian Tribes, individual Indians, and Alaska Natives by providing direct budget, planning, and administrative support, including oversight of contracts for human resources, acquisition, and financial/accounting services efficiently and effectively. Reports to the Department, the Office of Management and Budget, and to the U.S. Congress are generated by, or coordinated through this office.

Functions of the BF&A program include coordination of government-wide, Departmental, and other agency services that support OST's programs such as: personnel, EEO, space, telephone, charge card, travel system, vehicle management, and working capital fund activities. The office also handles the processing and mailing of Individual Indian Money (IIM) account holder checks, oil and gas Explanation of Payments, Statements of Performance, and other beneficiary related documents.

In addition, BF&A coordinates the implementation of performance improvement, human capital and transportation management. Recent accomplishments include: implementation of a Telework Program and coordination of the conversion to the Financial and Business Management System (FBMS).

Litigation Support ($3,986,000) – The budget for BF&A includes funding for the Solicitor's to provide document production capabilities for tribal trust litigation cases and caseload management efforts.

Office of Hearings and Appeals ($8,716,000) - The budget for BF&A includes funding for the Office of Hearings and Appeals for probate adjudication. Although the responsibility for directing overall probate efforts rests with BIA, OST oversees caseload management efforts; ensures coordination of policies, practices and systems; and provides guidance in identifying problems and potential solutions to case processing bottlenecks.

OHA Probate Performance Data 2012-2014				
	Number of Cases Pending Beginning of Year	Number of New Cases Received	Number of Cases decided	Number of Cases Pending End of Year
FY 2012	5,610	7,733	7,412	5,931
FY 2013	5,931	7,000	7,000	5,931
FY 2014	5,931	7,000	7,000	5,931

2014 Program Performance

- Support the Individual Indian Money Account Litigation Settlement Land Buy-Back program by mailing out tens of thousands of offers to purchase fractionated land.
- Improve budget-performance integration by defining correlations between available resources and performance for OST programs.
- Conduct management meetings to discuss performance accomplishments and budget resources necessary for improvements and realignment of funds as required.
- Continue mailing Explanation of Payment (EOP) statements and advice notices to beneficiaries.
- Continue processing and mailing beneficiary checks timely and accurately.
- Continue mailing tribal and individual Statements of Performance for accounts and tax forms.
- Continue mailing invoices and 1099's (Miscellaneous Income.)
- Maintain annual review of the budgetary status of trust accounts.
- Continue providing Human Resources, Acquisitions, and Finance services through shared service providers.
- Continue providing office space and Working Capital Fund service.

Information Resources ($6,599,000/35 FTE) - The Office of Information Resources (IR) through the Assistant Director for Information Resources (ADIR) provides organization-wide information resources support for OST in carrying out the fiduciary trust responsibilities to tribal and individual Indian beneficiaries; develops, maintains, and operates the trust information technology (IT) enterprise architecture; provides day-to-day computer support to OST personnel nationwide; and develops and maintains applications in support of the OST mission.

In addition, the ADIR oversees and directs IT support services including technical support, capital planning, and procurement of IT hardware and software; security management (accreditation and authorization, logical access control, policies, procedures, guidelines and compliance); and OST's implementation of DOI's IT Transformation initiatives. The ADIR facilitates the development and maintenance of cost-effective, supportable, and sustainable information management and technology solutions to advance the mission of OST. These technology solutions enhance OST's ability to serve the beneficiaries through efficient business and resource management systems.

The ADIR interfaces with the Departmental CIO office on strategic initiatives, department-wide planning, and IT Transformation activities. The ADIR develops IT strategic plans to support OST business processes; manages OST's IT services which provide the daily OST data systems' support, testing and implementation of automated trust funds financial and other support systems; and ensures necessary interfaces with other trust systems in the BIA, Bureau of Safety and Environmental Enforcement (BSEE), OHA, BLM, ONRR, and other related offices in the Department.

Office of External Affairs ($1,620,000/9 FTE) - OEA has three primary areas of responsibility in supporting the Special Trustee's statutorily-required reform and oversight activities: (1) communicating with a diverse group of stakeholders about OST's programs and activities and the Department's trust reform initiatives; (2) administration of OST's tribal self-governance and self-determination program; and (3) congressional liaison activities.

Communications - OEA provides tribal and individual Indian trust beneficiaries, Department personnel, the media, the U.S. Congress, other government agencies, and the public with a wide range of information on the status of trust reform priorities, current initiatives and benefits through personal contacts and printed materials. The Reform Act authorizes Tribes to withdraw tribal funds held in trust status for tribal self-investment and management, thereby eliminating federal management. To withdraw tribal funds, a Tribe must submit an application that includes data and information about how the Tribe intends to invest and manage the funds once withdrawn from trust status. OEA provides information to Tribes on the withdrawal process and coordinates OST's activities in response requests for withdrawal.

OEA can assist Tribes, if requested, to obtain technical assistance during the development of a trust withdrawal application. After OEA and appropriate OST subject matter experts determine that the application is complete, the regulations provide that OST has 90 days to review and approve or decline the application. The regulations allow additional time for information or clarifications to be received during the review process.

<u>Self-governance and Self-determination</u> - Staff provide information to Tribes on self-governance and self-determination opportunities under P.L. 93-638, and provide technical assistance to encourage Tribes to consider contracting or compacting OST programs. To ensure fulfillment of the Secretary's fiduciary trust responsibilities, staff actively pursue the negotiation of program standards with Tribes electing to contract or compact OST programs.

A significant portion of OEA's operating budget is used to support the administration of Indian self-governance and self-determination activities as authorized by Title I and Title IV of Public Law 93-638. In FY 2012, OEA worked with over 38 Tribes that performed or sought to perform OST programs and functions on behalf of their members, and worked to ensure Tribes had program standards for the performance of OST functions in place. OEA continues to assist Tribes in support of self-determination and self-governance and to provide opportunities for new Tribes interested in operating OST trust programs or seeking authority to access OST IR-based trust systems.

<u>Congressional Liaison</u> - In fulfillment of congressional liaison responsibilities, OEA provides the Congress with a range of information on the status of trust reform priorities, current initiatives and benefits through formal briefings, personal contacts, and printed materials.

2014 Program Performance

In FY 2014, OEA will promote Tribal self-determination and self-governance by seeking expanded participation in tribal operation of OST programs. OEA will provide information to Tribes currently operating OST trust programs to assist them in accessing OST's trust systems at their tribal facility.

OEA will support self-governance and self-determination by:
- Administering the full range of P.L. 93-638 self-governance and self-determination activities and services to include: promoting opportunities; providing technical assistance; developing tribal share packages; negotiating, approving or declining P.L. 93-638 contract proposals; negotiating program standards; negotiating Funding Agreements; negotiating Reprogramming Requests and footnotes; and coordinating the allocation of OST 638 funds to BIA and the Office of Self-Governance.
- Negotiating annual funding agreements, memoranda of understanding, and tribal use agreements and program standards for the compacting/contracting available OST programs.
- Holding discussions with requesting Tribes to share information about potential access to OST IR-based trust systems.
- Coordinating cost determinations for Tribes to access OST IR-based trust systems.
- Coordinating the approval process for any tribal requests to access OST IR-based trust systems.
- Coordinating activities within BIA and OST to provide OST trust systems training for Tribes.

OEA will support communications to stakeholders by:
- Continuing the proactive development of communications and media materials.
- Continuing support of OST's national debit card and direct deposit programs for IIM account holders.
- Enhancing OST's relationship with national and local media.
- Continuing communications with Members of Congress and their staff to discuss trust reform initiatives and potential legislative solutions.

- Continuing to provide written updates to Congress and Tribal Leaders on the status of trust reforms.
- Coordinating and reviewing formal applications from Tribes to withdraw their funds from trust status, for tribal self-investment and management and encouraging enhanced tribal involvement in this program whenever possible.

Activity: Program Operations and Support
Subactivity: Program Support – Program Management

	2013 Full Year CR	2012 Enacted	Fixed Costs & Related Changes (+/-)	Internal Transfers (+/-)	Program Changes (+/-)	2014 Request	Change from 2012 Enacted (+/-)
Program Management	*12,857*	**17,619**	**94**	**-3,806**	**+1,556**	**15,463**	**-2,156**
Trust Review & Audit	*2,209*	4,677	+25	-1,565	+1,802	4,939	+262
Risk Management	*637*			+637		637	+637
Trust Records	*10,011*	12,942	+69	-2,878	-246	9,887	-3,055
FTE	*110*	109	+0	+0	+3	112	3

Summary of 2014 Program Changes for Program Support - Program Management

Request Component	($000)	FTE
Program Changes:		
Increase for program operations.	+1,802	+3
Savings in program efficiencies	-246	+0
TOTAL Program Changes	**+1,556**	**+3**

Justification of 2014 Program Changes

The FY 2014 budget request for Program Management is $15,463,000 and 112 FTE, a net program increase of $1,556,000 and +3 FTE from the 2012 enacted budget.

Internal transfers include:
- -$3,986,000 from the Office of Trust Records to Budget, Finance, and Administration for the Department's Office of the Solicitor and +$1,108,000 to the Office of Trust Records from Historical Trust Accounting for records storage space, resulting in a net transfer of $2,878,000.
- +$637,000 from Trust Accountability for the Risk Management Division to Program Management, and -$1,565,000 from Trust Review and Audit to fund support staff in Business Management, for a net transfer of -$928,000.

Program Enhancement (+$1,802,000/+3 FTE) – In FY 2014, a program increase of $1,802,000 and +3 FTE is proposed for the Trust Review and Audit program. Additional funding is requested to increase the number of examinations performed by adding auditors. In recognition of the increased scope of responsibilities resulting from the transfer of the Risk Management function to this program, and as part of OST's realignment, two additional positions were added in FY2013—a Deputy Special Trustee and a support staff.

Program Reduction (-$246,000/0 FTE) – In FY 2014 a program decrease of -$246,000 is proposed for the Office of Trust Records as a result of increases in efficiency and decreases in service costs at the American Indian Records Repository.

Program Overview

Three separate functional units comprise Program Management: the Office of Trust Records, Trust Review and Audit, and Risk Management. All three report to the Deputy Special Trustee of Program Management and support OST in carrying out the fiduciary trust responsibilities to tribal and individual Indian beneficiaries. Trust Review and Audit provides independent audits of Indian fiduciary trust programs and monitors implementation of corrective actions to address any deficiencies. Risk Management operates a comprehensive risk management service to identify and mitigate risk. The Office of Trust Records (OTR) manages the operations of the American Indian Records Repository. Tangent to the management of records, OTR is responsible for the development of records management policies, and providing records management training and support services to OST and Indian Affairs.

Office of Trust Review and Audit ($4,939,000/26 FTE) The Office of Trust Review and Audit (OTRA) reports directly to the Deputy Special Trustee – Program Management, who in turn reports to the Principal Deputy Special Trustee for American Indians.

The Trust Reform Act states the Special Trustee shall oversee all reform efforts within OST, the Bureau of Indian Affairs (BIA), the Bureau of Land Management (BLM), and the Office of Natural Resources Revenue (ONRR) to ensure compliance with the Indian Trust Reform Act. OTRA will conduct Generally Accepted Government Auditing Standards compliant audits at OST, BIA, BLM, and ONRR. The purpose of these audits will be to determine if the OST, BIA, BLM and ONRR have established and are complying with appropriate policies and procedures, and developed necessary systems that will allow management of the fiduciary trust assets consistent with statutory requirements.

OTRA conducts examinations, identifies deficiencies, coordinates findings, generates reports, and monitors corrective actions for trust programs and records management assessments, including the evaluation of tribally-managed trust programs compacted with the Department of the Interior. OTRA also conducts special reviews at the request of Department officials, beneficiaries, or the public. In addition, OTRA funds a contract that conducts the annual financial trust funds audit that is performed by independent external auditors.

OTRA work activities support OST's trust reform goals to improve beneficiary services, Indian trust ownership, management of land and natural resources, management of trust fund assets, and support Indian self-governance and self-determination. Streamlining of processes and improvement of the efficiency of operations is supported through monitoring the reviews performed of Indian trust asset management activities Department-wide, providing timely reports and recommendations to Departmental senior management on efficiency and effectiveness of operations, compliance with applicable laws and regulations at the program and/or field office level.

The Indian Trust Rating System (ITRS) was developed to provide a method for assessing the operational effectiveness of Indian trust asset management activities Department-wide. The ITRS provides a methodology for assessing the overall effectiveness and performance based on: (1) Management - the capabilities and quality of management, (2) Asset Management - management of Indian trust assets, (3)

Compliance - compliance with applicable laws, regulations, policies, procedures, and accepted standards of fiduciary conduct, and (4) Operations - effectiveness and efficiency of operations, including the adequacy and effectiveness of internal controls.

To comply with the mandates of the *American Indian Trust Fund Management Reform Act of 1994,* OST conducts an Indian trust examination process to assist the Department and participating Tribes in the management of Indian trust operations and programs. The results of these examinations are provided to the managers of Indian trust programs and Indian fiduciary activities at the tribal and federal levels to address deficiencies and improve overall trust operations and management. Due to the comprehensive nature of the Indian trust examinations and the increasing number of trust programs that must be evaluated, these examinations are prioritized by trust rating, risk factors, or exam cycle.

In FY 2014, OTRA anticipates increasing its current exam workload to include reviews of the Office of Appraisal Services and potentially the Land Buy-Back Program, as a result of the implementation of the Individual Indian Money Account Litigation Settlement. A conservative estimate of ten additional examinations has been added to the OTRA workload for the FY 2014 trust examination goals.

Records Management Assessments (180 sites)	2012 Actual	2013 Estimate	2014 Estimate
Number of sites reviewed	45	50	60

Trust Examinations (180 sites)	2012 Actual	2013 Estimate	2014 Request
Number of sites reviewed	53	50	55

Risk Management ($637,000/5 FTE): The Office Risk Management (ORM) was realigned from Trust Accountability to report to the Deputy Special Trustee – Program Management (DST-PM) on November 30, 2012. The purpose for the realignment was to provide better customer service and to streamline the reporting process for risk management activities. Aligning ORM under the DST-PM also results in ORM receiving timely executive management guidance/direction in fulfilling their risk management activities/responsibilities. Receiving timely executive management guidance/direction is critical to ensure adverse or problematic issues, identified while fulfilling risk management activities/responsibilities, are timely and appropriately addressed/rectified.

The ORM continues to be proactive through identification of risk associated with program activities and implementation of controls to mitigate identified risk. All OST offices conduct risk assessments to evaluate the effectiveness of internal controls. OST's ORM ensures that among the program manager risk assessments, the reviews conducted by OTRA and independent external auditors, OST management can provide reasonable assurance that the financial reports are reliable, their programs are operating efficiently and effectively, and their programs are in compliance with applicable laws and regulations. OST will continue to strengthen its risk management program by: increasing the quantity of field locations tested; improving OST staff expertise based on offering of risk management training to OST staff; increasing support of internal programs and internal control testing efforts across bureaus more efficiently; enhancing the existing risk management tool (RM-PLUS) to facilitate more efficient assessing and reporting; and continued alignment of RM-PLUS with regulatory and legislative requirements, in particular, OMB Circular A-123, with Appendices, and Federal Managers Financial Integrity Act. ORM also collaborates with other bureaus and offices that provide trust services impacting OST's trust operations and trust fund financial statements.

Risk Management - Performance Data	2012 Actual	2013 Estimate	2014 Estimate
Number of Program Self-Assessments Performed in Automated Tool (RM-Plus)	48	44	44
Number of Programs Tested	40	38	31

2014 Program Performance

- Prepare Indian Trust Examinations and Tribal Trust Evaluations using an audit software solution to streamline the Trust Examination process,
- Leverage information technology in the distribution of OTRA final reports.
- Implement statistical sampling techniques and methodologies in audit planning and performance.
- Collaborate with the BIA in using interdisciplinary teams to evaluate the most complex Trust programs.
- Achieve Certified Government Auditing Professional certifications for OTRA auditors.
- Apply the comprehensive Indian Trust Rating System to all entities evaluated.
- Track and report on examination findings, recommendations and corrective action plans for all examinees.
- Perform quarterly follow-up on corrective action plans for records management assessments.
- Collaborate and coordinate closure of all OST findings and recommendations received from external audit entities. Continue efforts to improve efficiency by seeking ways to streamline the trust examination process.
- Perform audit liaison activities for the OST annual financial trust funds audit. Ensure examinations are performed in accordance with General Accepted Government Auditing Standards and the "Quality Standards for Inspections" issued by the Council of Inspectors General on Integrity and Efficiency.
- Development of an OTRA Standard Operating Procedures Manual to ensure standardization and consistency of work performance.
- Ensure all OTRA employees complete, every two years, at least 80 hours of continuing professional education that enhance their professional proficiency to perform examinations.
- Perform interim testing more timely and increase the coverage of field locations tested within a program.
- Increase the volume of programs documented or updated each year to reflect organizational and operational changes.
- Perform quarterly monitoring of RM-PLUS open corrective action plans.
- Continue initiatives, such as training and implementation and dissemination of a Risk Management Handbook, to ensure management has a clear understanding of the nature and types of risks, the internal controls designed to mitigate those risks, and their role in assuring the effectiveness of those internal controls.

- Collaborate with other Departmental offices to validate and/or leverage management control reviews outlined in the Office of Management and Budget Circular A-123

Office of Trust Records ($9,887,000/81FTE): The Office of Trust Records (OTR) reports directly to the Deputy Special Trustee – Program Management (DST-PM), who in turn reports to the Principal Deputy Special Trustee for American Indians. OTR is comprised of two Divisions: (1) the Division of Records Management Operations which is responsible for the management and operations of the American Indian Records Repository (AIRR) located in Lenexa, Kansas and (2) the Division of Records Management Policies, Procedures, and Training which is responsible for the development of records management policies/procedures, providing records management training, and providing records management support services to OST, Bureau of Indian Affairs (BIA), Bureau of Indian Education (BIE), and Assistant Secretary – Indian Affairs (AS-IA) personnel.

OTR is responsible for the management of OST, BIA, BIE, and AS-IA records programs by providing guidance and support on records management. OTR is responsible for development of, and obtaining approval from the Archivist of the United States, for records schedules; supporting computer-based records management training; disposition and safeguarding of inactive records; retrieval of records for authorized users; and supporting the implementation of the Departmental eMail Enterprise

Entrance to the American Indian Records Repository

Records and Document Management System (eERDMS). OTR will also provide records management training and technical assistance to Tribes/Consortia requesting such services and collaborate with the Tribes/Consortia in the development of a Tribal/Consortia records management program.

OTR developed and utilizes the Box Index Search System (BISS), a searchable electronic database of all Indian records in AIRR. This electronic database contains information on all boxes of inactive records retired at AIRR.

OTR support for inactive records includes: maintaining and updating retired records in the BISS; ensuring that the necessary security safeguards remain in place at the AIRR; prohibiting the withdrawal of original records from AIRR; preserving and providing remediation services for inactive records received at AIRR; and providing access for research purposes to authorized users of the records.

Records Management Performance Data	2012 Actual	2013 Estimate	2014 Estimate
Number of Personnel Trained – On-line	401	400	400
Number of Boxes stored	12,531	12,600	12,600

Note: FY 2013 and FY 2014 number of boxes stored are estimates based on an average of prior years.

TAB INSERT

Trust Funds

Tribal and Other Trust Funds

(Dollars in Thousands)

	2013 Full Year CR	2012 Enacted	Fixed Costs & Related Changes (+/-)	Internal Transfers (+/-)	Program Changes (+/-)	2014 Request	Change from 2012 Enacted (+/-)
Total	*413,163*	**428,754**	**+0**	**+0**	**-879**	**427,875**	**-879**
Tribal Special Fund	*313,157*	328,324	+0	+0	-4,302	324,022	-4,302
Tribal Trust Fund	*100,006*	100,430	+0	+0	+3,423	103,853	+3,423
FTE	*0*	0	+0	+0	+0	0	+0

Summary of 2014 Program Changes for Trust Funds

Request Component	($000)	FTE
Program Changes:		
Tribal Special Fund	-4,302	**0**
Tribal Trust Fund	+3,423	**0**
TOTAL Program Changes	**-879**	**0**

Justification of 2014 Program Changes

The 2014 budget request for the Tribal Special Fund and Tribal Trust Fund totals $427,875,000, a program decrease of -$879,000 from the 2012 enacted receipts and outlays.

The budget authority for the Tribal Special Fund and Tribal Trust Fund is equal to receipts of settlements and/or judgments from the Judgment Funds for on-budget trust funds as well as transaction activity from buying and selling investments outside of Treasury for on-budget trust funds; including investment income and proceeds from investment in government sponsored entity securities. Most of the assets of these funds are in investments held outside Treasury.

Budgetary Classification of Tribal Trust Funds

Tribal trust funds are deposited into consolidated accounts in the U.S. Treasury pursuant to: 1) general or specific acts of Congress and, 2) Federal management of tribal real properties, the titles to which are held in trust for the Tribes by the United States. These funds are available to the respective tribal groups for various purposes, under various acts of Congress, and may be subject to the provisions of tribal constitutions, bylaws, charters, and resolutions of the various Tribes, bands, or groups.

Commencing with FY 2000, most tribal trust funds, including special funds, managed by the Office of the Special Trustee were reclassified as non-budgetary. Ownership of these funds did not change; changes were made for presentation purposes only. Some tribal trust funds remain budgetary, in the Tribal Special or Tribal Trust Funds accounts.

The budgetary funds are included in either a budgetary special fund account or trust fund account. The distinction between a special and a trust fund is purely technical from a budgetary standpoint; if the law creating the fund delineates it as a "trust fund," it is included in the trust fund account. If the law delineates the fund as something other than a trust fund (e.g., a "development fund") it is included in the special fund account.

Tribal Special Fund

This fund includes activities associated with the following accounts:

- *Tribal Economic Recovery Fund.* This fund is authorized by the Three Affiliated Tribes and *Standing Rock Sioux Tribe Equitable Compensation Act of 1992* (P.L. 102-575) and holds funds which have been appropriated pursuant to the Act. Beginning in 1998, interest earned on the principal of this fund is available for both Tribes for economic development, education, and social services programs.
- *Three Affiliated Fort Berthold* (P.L. 102-575). The fund is not designated by law as a trust fund. The act provides for additional compensation to the Three Affiliated Tribes and the Standing Rock Sioux Tribe for the taking of tribal lands related to the Garrison Dam and Reservoir project. The Tribes are only entitled to the interest earnings, not the corpus (Sec. 3504(a) (4)).
- *Standing Rock* (P.L. 102-575, Title XXXV). The Act provides for additional compensation to the Three Affiliated Tribes and the Standing Rock Sioux Tribe for the taking of tribal lands related to the Garrison Dam and Reservoir project. The Tribes are only entitled to the interest earnings, not the corpus (Sec. 3504(a) (4).
- *Papago Cooperative Fund* (P.L. 97-293). The fund was established for the Tribe to obtain services that are financed by earnings on investment of the fund.
- *Ute Tribe* (P.L. 102-575, Title V). The fund was established for certain environmental and developmental purposes. One of the expressed purposes of this act is to put the Tribe in the same economic position it would have been had features contemplated by a September 20, 1965 agreement with the United States and others been constructed and thus, resolve tribal claims arising out of the agreement. In addition, the Act qualifies the Tribe's reserved rights and provides for the waiver of tribal claims related to this issue. The funds provided for by Section 504, like all funds provided for by the Act, with the exception of those funds provided for under Section 505, are intended to resolve legal claims related to the Tribe's water rights.
- *Pyramid Lake Indian Reservation* (P.L. 101-618). (Specifically, the Lahonta Valley and Pyramid Lake Fish and Wildlife Fund). The Lahonta Valley and Pyramid Lake Fish and Wildlife Fund consist of payments for the use of certain water and transfers from the Fisheries Fund. Except for the transfers, the use of the funds is subject to appropriations for fish and protection.
- *San Luis Rey Water Authority* (P.L. 100-675). This is settlement legislation that resolves pending water rights litigation between the United States and the Bands local entities. The Act established the San Luis Rey Tribal Development Fund and authorized appropriations of $30 million to the Fund. Following execution of the proposed settlement agreement, the Secretary of the Treasury is directed to make the funds available upon the request of the Indian Water Authority.
- *Cochiti Wetfields Solution.* In 1994, the Army Corps of Engineers transferred $4 million pursuant to P.L. 102-358 to fund the Department's responsibilities under the settlement agreement between Cochiti Tribe, the Corps, and the Department. The Secretary of the Interior is responsible for

maintenance, repair, and replacement of a drainage system constructed by the Corps for the Cochiti Pueblo.

Tribal Trust Fund

This fund includes activities associated with the following accounts:

- *Funds Contributed for the Advancement of the Indian Race.* This fund accounts for any contributions, donations, gifts, etc., which are to be used for the benefit of American Indians in accordance with the donors' wishes (82 Stat. 171).
- *Bequest of George C. Edgeter.* This fund includes a donation made by George C. Edgeter; income is available according to the terms of the bequest for the expenditure as determined by the Assistant Secretary, Indian Affairs for the relief of American Indians.
- *Ella M. Franklin Fund.* This fund consists of a bequest, the principal of which is invested in U.S. Treasury securities, and the interest is to be used for the relief of American Indians as specified by the donors' wishes (82 Stat. 171).
- *Josephine Lambert Fund.* This fund includes a donation made by Josephine Lambert, income to be used for the health or education of underprivileged Indian children.
- *Orrie Shaw Fund.* This fund includes a donation made by Dr. Orrie Shaw, income used only for the training or education of American Indians.
- *Welmas Endowment Fund.* This fund was established to receive revenue generated by land owned by the decedent for the period of ten (10) years whereby the annual interest earnings of the endowment can be distributed by the Assistant Secretary Indian Affairs for the education of members of federally recognized Tribes; provided that 20 percent of the annual interest serves to benefit the education of Agua Caliente Tribal members. The Tribe has the option of obtaining complete control of the land, prior to the end of the endowment period, if it elects to fund the endowment so that the principal amount reaches $750,000.
- *Arizona Intertribal Fund* (P.L. 100-696). The fund represents an exchange agreement for privately held lands in Florida for publicly held land in Arizona. Use of the money is subject to appropriations and is available to pay for supplemental education and child welfare programs.
- *Navajo Trust Fund* (P.L. 100-696). The fund ratifies an exchange of Federal land in Arizona.
- *Crow Creek* (P.L. 104-223). The Act established a corpus that is to be invested and makes the interest earnings available without appropriation for the various activities under Section 5. However, the Act does not appear to transfer ownership of the money to the Tribe or create a legal claim to the funds, until it is paid to them.
- *Lower Brule Infrastructure* (P.L. 105-132). The Act provides additional compensation to the Lower Brule Sioux Tribe for the taking of land related to the construction of the Fort Randall and Big Bend dams. The Congress had originally provided compensation of $4.3 million in 1958 and 1962. Total deposits capped at $39.3 million. The Act does not appear to transfer ownership of the money to the Tribe or create a legal claim to the funds, until it is paid to them.
- *Southern Ute Tribal Resource Fund* (P.L. 106-554). This fund was established in FY 2002. As part of the requirements under Section 18 of the Act for disbursing the tribal resource funds, the Colorado Ute are required to submit a resource acquisition and enhancement plan or an investment plan to the Secretary for approval.

- *Ute Mountain Tribal Resource Fund* (P.L. 106-554). The fund was established in FY 2002. As part of the requirements under Section 18 of the Act for disbursing the tribal resource funds, the Colorado Ute are required to submit a resource acquisition and enhancement plan or an investment plan to the Secretary for approval.

- *Chippewa Cree Tribal Compact ADM/Chippewa Cree Future Water Supply* (P.L. 106-163). The fund was established in FY 2001. The trust fund is established under Title I, Sec. 104, Chippewa Cree Indian Reserved Water Rights Settlement Trust Fund. The ownership of the trust fund does not convey to the Tribe until such time as the Tribe waives all claims and meets the underlying settlement requirements.

- *Shivwits Band of Paiute Indians* (P.L. 106-263). The fund was established in FY 2002. Ownership of the trust fund does not convey to the Tribe until such time as funds have been appropriated and deposited into the Trust fund; the St. George Water Reuse Project Agreement, the Santa Clara Project Agreement and the Settlement Agreement are approved and in effect; the State Engineer of Utah has approved all applications necessary to implement the provision of the Santa Clara Project Agreement, St. George Water Reuse Agreement and the Settlement Agreement; the Court has entered a judgment and decree confirming the Shivwits Water Rights and is final as to all parties to the Santa Clara Division and the Virgin River Adjudication.

- *Northern Cheyenne Indian Reserved Water Rights Settlement Trust Fund* (P.L. 103-374). This fund established a $21.5 million trust fund for the Northern Cheyenne Indian Tribe. These funds may be used by the Tribe to make $11.5 million available to the State of Montana as a loan to assist in financing Tongue River Dam project costs; land and natural resources administration, planning, and development; land acquisition; and any other purpose determined by the Tribe. In addition, this fund holds $31.5 million for the enlargement and repair of the Tongue River Dam project.

- *The Crow Creek Sioux Tribe Infrastructure Development Trust Fund of 1996* (P.L. 104-223, 110 Stat 3026). The fund establishes a Crow Creek Sioux Tribe Infrastructure Development Trust Fund. In FY 1997, $27.5 million was deposited into the Fund. The interest earned from the invested principal is available for payment to the Tribe for tribal educational, health care, recreational, and other projects.

TAB INSERT

Fiscal Year 2012 Annual Report to Congress

Office of the Special Trustee
for American Indians
Fiscal Year 2012 Annual Report to Congress

United States Department of the Interior
Office of Special Trustee for American Indians
Washington, D.C. 20240

March 18, 2013

Dear Member of Congress:

I am pleased to provide the Office of the Special Trustee for American Indians (OST) fiscal year (FY) 2012 annual report to Congress pursuant to the requirements stated in 25 U.S.C. § 4043 (f). The report presents OST's ongoing actions to improve services to tribal and individual Indian trust beneficiaries.

Returning to OST in 2011 after having served as the OST Chief of Staff until 2005, I had the opportunity to oversee significant changes in operations.

OST's support of the **Secretarial Commission on Indian Trust Administration and Reform** and preparation for trust land consolidation through the **Land Buy-Back Program** drove much activity in FY2012. The report explains how OST developed **OASIS**, an electronic appraisal request preparation, tracking, and reporting system, and **MAPS**, a system to estimate fair market value and fair annual rents, to facilitate the Buy-Back Program. OST also prioritized resolution of account data discrepancies to support *Cobell* **Settlement payments**. Both the Commission and the Buy-Back Program were referenced in the terms of the *Cobell* Settlement, Title I of the *Claims Resolution Act of 2010*.

Partnerships with the Bureau of Indian Affairs and other bureaus and offices within Interior, federal and state agencies, and tribal leaders and organizations improved the quality of our services. Of particular note was the creation of interagency agreements between the **Department of the Treasury** and OST. Read in the report about why Treasury selected OST to expertly invest millions of dollars of tribal funds.

Beneficiaries responded enthusiastically to implementation of **electronic notifications**. Individual Indian Money beneficiaries who use direct deposit or a debit card were offered deposit notifications via text message or email, instead of by regular mail. Besides providing safety and convenience for beneficiaries, e-notifications save the government printing and postage costs. The report looks at the implementation of this very successful effort, despite the digital divide that exists in Indian Country.

I welcome your feedback on these efforts and other content in this report. Please contact my office at 202-208-4866 for additional information about OST and the Indian trust.

Sincerely,

Michele F. Singer
Principal Deputy Special Trustee

Office of the Special Trustee for American Indians
Annual Report to Congress - Fiscal Year 2012

The Office of the Special Trustee for American Indians (OST) was established by the *American Indian Trust Fund Management Reform Act of 1994*, Public Law 103-412 (Reform Act). The office was created to improve the accountability and management of Indian funds held in trust by the federal government. As trustee, the Department of the Interior (Interior) has the primary fiduciary responsibility to manage tribal trust funds and Individual Indian Money (IIM) accounts, as well as resources that generate income for those accounts.

The Indian trust consists of 55 million surface acres and 57 million acres of subsurface minerals estates held in trust by the United States for American Indians, Indian tribes, and Alaska Natives. Over 11 million acres belong to individual Indians and nearly 44 million acres are held in trust for Indian tribes. On these lands, the department manages over 119,000 leases. It also manages more than $4 billion in trust funds. For fiscal year (FY) 2012, income from financial assets and from leases, settlements and judgments, use permits, and land sales, totaling approximately $487 million, was collected for about 387,000 open IIM accounts. Approximately $1.4 billion was collected in FY2012 for about 3,000 tribal accounts (for over 250 tribes).

A Unique Trust

The status of the Indian trust is unlike other trusts. Beyond size, other factors make the Indian trust unique.

The Indian trust gradually evolved from a series of Congressional actions — beginning with the *General Allotment Act of 1887* (Dawes Act) — and subsequent policy changes. No single trust document created the Indian trust to articulate the fiduciary duties incumbent on the federal government in managing that trust. In a commercial trust, such a document would provide specific guidance for the management of trust assets. Unlike the commercial trust environment, where accounts and underlying trust assets must remain economically viable and productive or face liquidation under the common law of trusts, a large number of small accounts exist within the Indian trust. Most Indian trust accounts would fall below the minimal threshold for commercial trust accounts.

The Indian fiduciary trust administered by Interior does not charge for services to manage the natural resources of the trust or the investment of trust funds. Virtually 100 percent of income is returned to tribes and individuals. The Bureau of Indian Affairs (BIA) is responsible for natural resource management. OST handles fiduciary assets. In many cases, the cultural heritage associated with a natural resource held in trust is more important to the beneficiary than its monetary worth.

Tribes are supported by OST if they choose to withdraw their trust funds. Subchapter II of the Reform Act addresses the voluntary withdrawal of trust funds by tribes. As stated in the law, the purpose of the subchapter is to provide tribes "an opportunity to manage tribal funds currently held in trust by the United States and managed by the Secretary through the Bureau, that, consistent with the trust responsibility of the United States and the principles of self-determination, will 1) give Indian tribal governments greater control over the management of such trust funds; or 2) otherwise demonstrate how the principles of self-determination can work with respect to the management of such trust funds, in a manner consistent with the trust responsibility of the United States." Under the Reform Act, from 1994 through FY2012, nine tribes have chosen to withdraw some or all of their trust funds out of trust status for self-management or investment.

Fractionation and Trust Land Consolidation

From the days of the first treaties to the present, there has been an effort to balance tribal and federal visions of the trust. One of the most controversial issues was passage of the Dawes Act. This act divided reservations by allotting a number of acres on the reservation to each Indian head of a family, single person, or orphan child. Land not allotted was deemed excess and was made available to settlers as fee land.

Many reservations have a checkerboard pattern of fee and trust lands, often as a result of the Dawes Act. The checkerboard effect has an impact on the economic viability of trust lands because laws that apply to fee lands and trust lands differ. Those seeking to lease the land for any purpose find their efforts further complicated if their dealings span both types of land ownership.

Deleterious effects of the Dawes Act have manifested in fractionated ownership of tracts of trust land. Often, when an original owner of an allotment passed away, ownership of the tracts was split among many family members. Each person inherited an *undivided interest* in the original tract. The process of increasing the number of owners of a tract, or *fractionation*, has continued for several generations. Today, many tracts have hundreds of owners. There is an economic impact of fractionation because 51 percent of a tract's owners need to agree before the land can be developed or used for such things as grazing, mineral extraction, or oil drilling. A tract with dozens of owners is at a disadvantage to reach consensus for use of the land, even if all the owners are able to be contacted.

There have been efforts in the past to reduce fractionation. Among them, the Indian Land Consolidation Act (ILCA) of 1983 (Public Law 97-459), as amended in 2000, authorized any tribe, with the Secretary's approval, to exchange or sell any tribal lands, or interest in lands, to eliminate undivided fractional interests in Indian trust or restricted lands or to consolidate tribal landholdings. The American Indian Probate Reform Act (AIPRA) of 2004 amended ILCA and changed the way trust estates were distributed to heirs. There have been subsequent amendments to AIPRA.

The *Claims Resolution Act of 2010* (Public Law 111-291) Title I, Individual Indian Money Account Litigation Settlement, is the most recent attempt to address fractionation. The act included the *Cobell* Settlement, which established the Trust Land Consolidation Fund. The settlement was finalized November 24, 2012. The fund provides $1.9 billion, over a ten-year period, to acquire fractionated interests in trust or restricted lands, up to 15 percent of the fund is available to implement a Land Buy-Back Program, and to pay costs related to the work of the Secretarial Commission on Indian Trust Administration and Reform.

Interior's Office of Valuation Services (OVS) and OAS collaborated in FY2012 to eliminate redundant valuations between the offices. The "One Appraisal Policy" avoids duplication of resources, shortens appraisal time, and controls costs.

Critical to land consolidation is the fair market valuation of property. OST's Office of Appraisal Services (OAS) has been working with other bureaus and offices in Interior to provide timely, reliable, and credible appraisal services in accordance with professional and federal standards.

Developed in-house and recognized as a significant asset to the land consolidation process, the **Office of Appraisal Services Information System (OASIS)** is an electronic appraisal request preparation, tracking, and reporting system. It streamlines creation of appraisal requests originated by the Bureau of Indian Affairs (BIA), the Office of Hearings and Appeals, or tribes for delivery to OAS. The system, implemented throughout OAS and BIA five months earlier than scheduled, provides status updates and produces various reports for coordination and reconciliation. Hard copies of appraisal requests have been eliminated, which saves personnel time and paper. Online training to over 300 OASIS users saved travel expenses and reduced labor costs. An OASIS webpage provides users with useful information and allows them to suggest improvements to OASIS. An updated version of OASIS is scheduled for release in FY2013.

OAS also created the **Mass Appraisal Program System (MAPS)**. MAPS is a system comprised of several mass appraisal methods, including an automated valuation model (AVM) used to estimate fair market value and fair annual rents. MAPS allows for a streamlined and quicker turnaround of appraisal requests, once upfront research and data systems are in place. It conforms to nationally recognized appraisal standards, *Uniform Standards of Professional Appraisal Practice and Uniform Appraisal Standards for Federal Land Acquisitions*, as applicable. MAPS is currently being used in several regions and broader application is planned. OAS regions using MAPS by the end of FY2012 included Eastern Oklahoma, Midwest, Northwest, and Great Plains.

The policy was successfully implemented among the Bureau of Reclamation (BOR), Bureau of Indian Affairs (BIA), and OAS on the Navajo/Gallup water project.

OAS also consulted with the U.S. Department of Agriculture (USDA), Army Corp of Engineers, Interior's Office of Hearings and Appeals (OHA), the Federal Highway Administration, OVS, BIA, and the departments of transportation of several states to establish uniform appraisal requirements and streamline appraisal processes. OAS worked with the Bureau of Land Management (BLM), OVS, and BIA to formulate processes to eliminate the development of duplicative data for real property appraisals. Establishment of a land consolidation website resulted in improved information sharing and overall project understanding.

OST signed a Memorandum of Understanding with OVS, BIA, and BLM on July 18, 2012, to correct mapping errors of fractionated land. OAS also implemented AgWare, market transaction data and report writing appraisal software, in the twelve OAS regional offices. OAS has linked market transaction data in AgWare with locational information on trust tracts/parcels stored in a geospatial information system database. This assists appraisers in developing appraisals, performing appraisal reviews, and providing real estate consulting services.

Such collaborations enhance the management and operation of the Buy-Back Program.

OST anticipated approval of the *Cobell* Settlement would instigate new workloads, not only for land consolidation but also for **Cobell payments**. During FY2012, OST worked with BIA, other federal entities, and contractors to provide current account holder information to Garden City Group, Inc., the claims administrator.

OST prioritized the clean-up of account holder discrepancies, resolving more than 99.98 percent of the original baseline discrepancies; over 13,000 items were resolved through the discrepancy review. The OST Trust Beneficiary Call Center responded to 9,721 IIM Account Litigation Settlement inquiries during FY2012.

The **Secretarial Commission on Indian Trust Administration and Reform** (Commission) was created to undertake a forward-looking, comprehensive evaluation of Interior's trust management of more than $4 billion in Native American trust assets. It held its first meeting March 2012. The Commission seeks input from affected individuals and tribes to identify opportunities to enhance Departmental accountability, responsiveness, and efficiency in the management of both natural resources and fiduciary assets.

OST has been supporting, and continues to support, Interior and the Commission. OST staff worked on all of the Commission's FY2012 public meetings and webinars, and hosted the June 2012 meeting held in Albuquerque. At each meeting, OST management made presentations. Dozens of background documents were provided on compact discs, and access to additional documents and other information was made available online to the Commission through OST's intranet. Secretary Salazar and Deputy Secretary Hayes requested that the Commission specifically consider OST's current and future trust responsibilities and functions as it evaluates Interior's trust management.

Operational Efficiencies

The following efforts were undertaken to advance beneficiary focus and participation while providing effective, competent stewardship and management of trust assets. As directed by Executive Order 13576, Delivering an Efficient, Effective, and Accountable Government, administrative cost savings and management efficiencies received critical attention in FY2012. All OST offices focused on their core operations to implement financial efficiencies, without impacting service to beneficiaries. Many of these efforts, if not most, rely upon robust partnerships and collaboration with BIA and other Interior offices and bureaus; federal, state and local agencies; and tribal organizations. Increasingly, OST is reaching out to communicate outside the organization in order to effect, enhance, or optimize outcomes of its internal efforts.

Saving Money

» Negotiated new agreements for annual acquisition and human resource services that saved $205,000 and $390,000, respectively

» Revised the contract for security services at OST's Albuquerque office, saving $138,000 annually

» Consolidated OST facilities at Lenexa, Kansas, reducing rent/utilities by approximately $200,000 annually; installed motion-activated light switches

» Discontinued an accounting services contract, saving $700,000 annually, and reorganized to provide the same function with current personnel, increasing employee morale and advancement opportunities, and establishing

O ver a ten-week period during the summer of 2012, Individual Indian Money beneficiaries who use direct deposit or a debit card were offered options to receive deposit notifications electronically (e-notifications), instead of by regular mail. The two new options were text message or email e-notifications.

E-notifications provide safety and convenience for beneficiaries. An e-notification is typically received by the beneficiary either the same day or the day after funds are credited to the individual's IIM account. A paper notification would have arrived several days after the deposit was made.

The offer was well-received. OST expects significant savings in printing and postage costs over the coming years as the use of e-notifications rises.

similar employee/supervisor ratios across branches and teams

» Relocated the OAS Eastern Oklahoma Regional Office with the BIA office to reduce space and to save approximately $65,000 annually on office rent

» Processed payment of a record $345 million Osage settlement one week earlier than required under the settlement agreement; over 3,900 direct deposits resulted in faster access to funds by beneficiaries and reduced transaction costs to the government

» Increased the number of beneficiaries who use electronic funds transfers, more than 6500 nationwide (958 debit card and 5,584 direct deposit), resulting in substantial direct savings to the government in transaction costs

» Initiated a pilot project, in collaboration with U.S Treasury and Chase Bank, for direct deposit

and debit card per capita payments in excess of $18 million to the Western Shoshone (check costs will be further reduced when this process is implemented for other tribal per capita and tribal credit payments)

» Increased online training, which reduced travel, printing, and shipping costs

» Processed and reconciled over 8.8 million financial transactions and approximately one million account maintenance transactions encompassing more than $1.9 billion in receipts and almost $1.3 billion in disbursements to individual Indian and tribal beneficiaries

Partnering for Results

» Prepared and issued FY 2012 audited financial statements on the IIM and tribal trust funds; the independent auditors, KPMG LLP, issued no material weaknesses

» Coordinated over 1,100 beneficiary outreach meetings throughout Indian Country and at off-reservation locations, such as the Phoenix and Chicago Indian centers; many involved cross-agency cooperation and coordination with other governmental organizations

» Participated in 2,400 meetings with tribal governments

» Provided over 260 separate trainings sessions to Indian youth and adults on fundamental financial skills training

» Provided enhanced monitoring to identify and track beneficiaries in need of social service

assistance, working with BIA and Office of the Solicitor (SOL) staff to implement; 501 IIM accounts were tracked

» Completed a "proof-of-concept" with the successful transmission and printing of beneficiary checks at the U.S. Department of the Treasury in a Continuity of Operations Plan (COOP) scenario

» Implemented Pay.gov, the Treasury's automatic direct deposit and credit card collection of payments for Bureau of Indian Affairs leases and permits, in September 2011 and received payments in FY2012 totaling $6,623,192.44

» Worked with BIA and DOI information technology staff to write a solicitation to see if a commercial, off-the-shelf system exists that would combine the functionality of the Trust Fund Accounting System (TFAS) and the Trust Asset and Accounting Management System (TAAMS)

» Partnered with BIA to review and close multiple forestry accounts, which reduced accounting and administrative costs

Operating Efficiently

» Automated and streamlined the liabilities payment process, saving over 1,000 staff hours annually

» Increased use of the TFAS Update Utility Program, which automates data entry, saving over 1,000 staff hours annually

» Implemented a process to upload bulk cash transactions via spreadsheet instead of manually keying individual transactions, saving over 2,000 staff hours annually

» Implemented the Per Capita Distribution System, automating the cash distribution process for verifying accounts and receipting per capita distributions from tribal accounts to numerous IIM supervised, whereabouts unknown, and estate accounts

» Processed 66,956 automated one-time disbursements, totaling in excess of $208 million

» Responded to 191,167 calls to the Trust Beneficiary Call Center

» Reduced the number of Whereabouts Unknown accounts (those

When the Department of the Treasury required investment services for various tribal funds created by legislation, they determined OST could expertly and cost effectively provide those services. Treasury determined that OST's costs were lower than hiring a contractor. Treasury also recognized OST's expertise in dealing with tribal governments and its well-established relationship with tribes.

After consultation with the tribes, **Treasury and OST entered into three Interagency Agreements** (IAAs) in FY2012 that allow OST to provide investment and program management services for the Cheyenne River Sioux Tribe, the Lower Brule Sioux Tribe, and the Crow Creek Tribe. Two more IAAs will be finalized in FY2013, while an additional two will continue to be negotiated.

OST's Trust Funds Investment division plans, develops, operates, and controls the buying, selling, and trading of investment instruments. The division provides technical advice and assistance to regional offices, agencies, and Indian tribes in developing financial plans and investment strategies for tribal trust funds. This is the expertise Treasury tapped, allowing OST to invest in eligible securities in accordance with the terms and conditions of the agreements.

lacking current address information on file with OST) by more than 18,800 (21.5%); aggregate value of the accounts made

with tribal statements to 5 minutes (previously 5 days), which allowed them to be produced on the same day as paper statements,

employees who did not chose the VERA-VSIP offer

» Promoted an ethical culture at OST by developing an ethics manual and training, providing one-on-one ethics orientation for new employees, creating a "one stop" location on OST's intranet for ethics information, emailing timely reminders and notices to all OST employees, and employing exit interview surveys

The Trust Beneficiary Call Center (TBCC) answered its **one millionth call** on May 17, 2012. TBCC opened its phone lines December 3, 2004. The well trained and patient personnel who answer the phones are available Monday through Friday from 7 a.m. to 6 p.m. and Saturday from 8 a.m. to noon, Mountain time.

More than 97 percent of callers have their questions answered during the call, which is referred to as first line resolution. (The industry standard is approximately 49 percent.) The remaining issues are escalated to OST staff. Those items are tracked by TBCC for follow up to ensure callers receive the information they request.

Information Technology (IT) Transformation Initiative

The IT Transformation initiative is a multi-year effort by Interior to reduce IT costs across the department and improve the effectiveness of IT services delivered to its employees. OST, led by its Assistant Director for Information Resources (ADIR), has been fully engaged in Interior's IT Transformation initiative.

available to IIM holders exceeded $21.4 million

» Disbursed $736,607 Special Deposit Account (SDA) funds using an in-house team of six, one third the number of personnel used in previous years (maximum historical amount disbursed annually by a staff of 18 was $1 million)

» Reconciled 425 return per capita accounts of which 212 accounts, cumulatively valued in excess of $2.8 million, were eligible for tribes to use under the newly developed Returned Per Capita Account Reconciliation System

» Provided OST staff and tribal representatives access to tribal account statements online
» Implemented a new process that reduced production of CDs

resulting in renewed tribal interest in electronic statement delivery

» Deployed 250 laptops that also function as in-office workstations to enable teleworking, which has increased employee productivity and satisfaction

» Developed an electronic Records Move Request (RMR) form, eliminated one level of RMR review, and implemented online approval and notification, streamlining the RMR process to save time and money; eliminated the backlog of RMRs pending legal reviews

» Offered Voluntary Early Retirement Authority (VERA) and Voluntary Separation Incentive Payment (VSIP) to 20 employees whose positions were eliminated; established a team that placed

In FY2012, OST made significant strides by developing and maintaining an OST server site migration plan that was included within the department's plan for Office of Management and Budget (OMB) review. During the year, OST virtualized over 80 percent of the OST server infrastructure in preparation for consolidation of OST data centers with BIA data centers. Virtualization allowed several physical servers to be changed to virtual machines on one of OST's physical servers, thereby reducing the footprint of OST's physical IT infrastructure. Virtualizing server infrastructure reduced electrical and cooling requirements, lowering those expenses. Forty percent of OST's production servers migrated to the BIA Albuquerque Data Center. OST also supported Interior's preparations for an agency-wide migration of the email system to a Google based system, referred to as BisonConnect.

Tribal Litigation

OST's Office of Historical Trust Accounting (OHTA) employees were part of an interagency workgroup that was tasked with determining a method to calculate amounts to use in settlement negotiations with tribes concerning claims about trust fund accounting and natural resource management. Other Interior and U.S. Department of Justice (DOJ) employees were also members of the workgroup.

A specialized group in OHTA, the tribal team, created Trust Account Databases (TADs) on an expedited basis as part of the settlement efforts. The team compiled and analyzed account data to create over 170 TADs for tribes. Information from six accounting systems and data sources were combined into each database that covered up to 64 years (July 1, 1946 to September 30, 2010) of trust fund activity. Trust Fund Expedited Settlement Evaluation Method calculations were run for over 100 tribes or tribal entities. In addition, technical papers, and work sessions and briefings with tribes, tribal officials, tribal consultants, tribal attorneys, and/or settlement judges were provided for approximately 90 tribes. Team members attended negotiations to provide tribes with expert explanations of the trust data.

Attorneys from DOJ and Interior's Office of the Solicitor formulated settlement offers after they considered the trust fund data and settlement analyses. Through FY2012, more than 50 tribal settlements were concluded. The combined value of those settlements exceeded $1

Financial skills are critical to building and managing personal wealth. OST, alone or in partnership with other private and public organizations, provides financial skills training that reaches Indian trust beneficiaries, and other community members, in Indian Country and in urban settings.

In FY2012, OST's **Field Operations** conducted or supported 136 **financial skills classes** for adults and 132 classes for youth. Participants included 1630 adults and 720 youth. Training materials, developed by the First Nations Development Institute, were designed specifically for Indian Country and include materials suitable for individuals at all levels of experience.

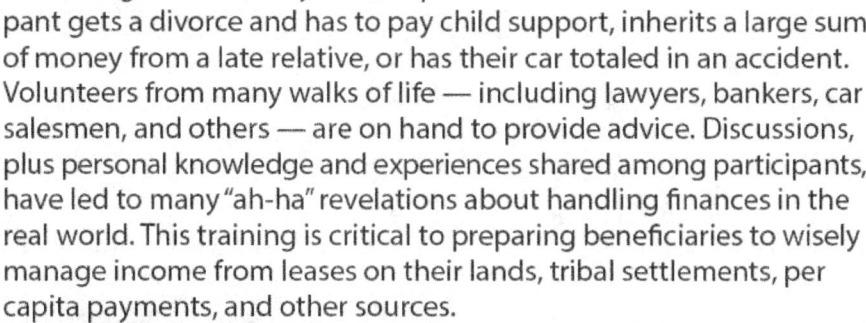

The classes combine instruction and experiential activities that engage participants about topics such as budgeting, investing, and planning for the future. The popular and effective Spending Frenzy exercise gives each participant a set amount of play money and a profile. Then participants make financial decisions based upon a given set of life challenges — both good and bad. The Fickle Finger of Fate may deem a participant gets a divorce and has to pay child support, inherits a large sum of money from a late relative, or has their car totaled in an accident. Volunteers from many walks of life — including lawyers, bankers, car salesmen, and others — are on hand to provide advice. Discussions, plus personal knowledge and experiences shared among participants, have led to many "ah-ha" revelations about handling finances in the real world. This training is critical to preparing beneficiaries to wisely manage income from leases on their lands, tribal settlements, per capita payments, and other sources.

billion. Additional tribes continue to negotiate with the government.

The settlements are important because of the potential for the funds to drive economic development in Indian Country. They also are bringing closure to historical grievances without costly litigation.

Tribal Consultation Initiative

On November 5, 2009, President Barack Obama issued a Presidential Memorandum directing each agency to submit a detailed plan of action describing how the agency will implement the policies and directives of Executive Order 13175. Interior established a joint federal-tribal team that developed a policy on tribal consultation. The policy includes elements that strive to honor the government-to-government relationship by

involving the appropriate level of decision maker in a consultation process, promoting innovations in communication by including a department-wide tribal governance officer (TGO), detailing early tribal involvement in the design of a process implicating tribal interests, and capturing a wide range of policy and decision making processes under the consultation umbrella.

Bureaus and offices, in collaboration with the TGO, were tasked to revise existing policies or develop new policies to conform to the department's policy. OST's tribal consultation policy team was established after Interior's policy was implemented December 1, 2011. Team members met with OST senior management to develop supplemental policy in areas unique to OST and to determine how implementation of the new policy might affect OST operations. The team continues to address this effort, working closely with Interior's TGO.

Efficiency Study Will Inform FY2013 Efforts

OST authorized an efficiency study, conducted by the vendor, Booz Allen Hamilton Inc. The results of the study, released April 30, 2012, offered quick wins and high impact recommendations. In response, OST's senior managers held several meetings to address better internal communications, an area the study highlighted. OST also responded to the study's recommendation to create a strategic plan by initiating a strategic planning process. The strategic plan will be completed in FY2013.

Among projects that will be pursued in FY2013 to specifically benefit beneficiaries while improving efficiency is a pilot project to provide IIM beneficiaries with real time online access to account information. Tribes already have this capability.

An effort to settle the Pembina litigation began in FY2012 and is expected to conclude in FY2013. OST has been working with BIA, SOL, and DOJ to identify per capita beneficiary listings in order to distribute the settlement funds.

Although Treasury is able to print beneficiary checks under a Continuity of Operations (COOP) situation, it lacks the ability to print beneficiary statements and explanations of payment. Therefore in FY2013, OST will continue its COOP effort by locating a third-party provider for this service.

Addressing issues of concern to employees is critical if OST is going to continue to be a high-functioning organization. This is especially true when an issue is safety related. To increase protection for OST field personnel, additional security measures were put in place for the OST office in Billings, Montana. Furthermore, arrangements were finalized to obtain space for the Billings' staff in a new federal building, which is under construction. The move to the new space will occur in FY2013. The new space will be outfitted with safety features, which cannot be added to the current space due to its historical designation. Additionally, the office space will be situated on the first floor to better accommodate beneficiaries who visit.

Conclusion

Offering more transparency for Indian trust beneficiaries to understand the sources and management of their funds, while protecting and increasing the value of those funds, are OST's top priorities. Each project undertaken has been, and will continue to be, benchmarked against those objectives. In addition, OST will continue to support Interior's work with the Secretarial Commission on Indian Trust Administration and Reform, the Land Buy-Back Program, and *Cobell* Settlement payments.

Every day, OST employees contribute their efforts to ensure fulfillment of the federal government's fiduciary obligation to tribal and individual Indian beneficiaries. They are proud to serve the government, the beneficiaries, and other stakeholders in this effort.

Images used on the cover through the inside back cover are from the Bureau of Indian Affairs (BIA) historical collection. The back cover image is licensed from Shutterstock, Inc. BIA images may be used with consent of the federal government. The Shutterstock image may not be reproduced.